For the English-language edition:

Translator
Trista Selous

Consultant
Dr Stuart K Monro
Scientific Director, Our Dynamic Earth
Principal Geologist, British Geological Survey

Editor
Camilla Rockwood

Prepress
Claire Williamson

Prepress manager
Sharon McTeir

Publishing manager
Patrick White

Originally published by Larousse as *Petit atlas des phénomènes naturels*
by Anne Debroise and Érick Seinandre

© Larousse/VUEF, 2003

English-language edition
© Chambers Harrap Publishers Ltd 2004

ISBN 0550 10157 8

Typeset by Chambers Harrap Publishers Ltd, Edinburgh
Printed in France by IME, Beaume-les-Dames

Anne Debroise and Érick Seinandre

Natural
Phenomena

CHAMBERS
World Library

Contents

Maps

Foreword

The planet is governed by natural phenomena, which may slowly shape its surface over millions of years or disturb it violently for a few seconds.

Such phenomena show us that the Earth is in a continual state of change. Its various constituents – the air mass, the ocean currents or the Earth's internal heat – interact with each other through feedback loops which maintain the Earth's system. These forces and interactions are becoming better understood, though much still has to be explored.

Natural phenomena can be a source of wonder: events such as eclipses, shooting stars, the aurora borealis and gigantic waterfalls can be particularly awesome. But they can also, understandably, provoke fear, as cyclones, tidal waves, volcanic eruptions or floods may cause devastation on a grand scale. Though we cannot control these events, we can certainly mitigate their effects. According to the latest meteorological predictions, global warming resulting from increased concentrations of greenhouse gases in the atmosphere may lead to a rise in the frequency of some natural disasters. While it is hard to gauge how far the most recent disasters are linked to any possible global warming, the cost of insuring against such risks has increased dramatically in recent years.

Although many of the processes that influence natural phenomena still remain unclear, our understanding of them has improved. Today, active volcanoes are closely monitored and the more lethal consequences of volcanic eruptions are more clearly understood, particularly those which may require the evacuation of local populations. The movements of cyclones and tsunamis are also monitored, again making it possible to warn the populations in their path to take precautions. Although as yet, we have no way of predicting earthquakes, construction techniques for earthquake-resistant buildings are improving. However, these advances are not enough to prevent the loss of human life and material damage which occurs when natural disasters affect the poorest regions of the planet.

A series of lightning bolts over a lake in the USA. This phenomenon occurs on Earth at an average rate of 100 times a second.

Volcanoes first appeared more than four thousand million years ago, when the Earth's crust began to solidify. The oceanic crust acts as a natural conduit, providing outlets for the heat that is created as radioactive elements in the planet's core decompose. Most volcanoes are concentrated on the edges of tectonic plates. When these plates move apart, rock rises to the surface from deep underground. Some volcanoes may also appear in the centre of a tectonic plate, while others occur where ocean is being subducted beneath younger continental crust, producing more violent volcanism. Volcanoes vary widely in appearance.

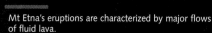

Mt Etna's eruptions are characterized by major flows of fluid lava.

A fiery Earth

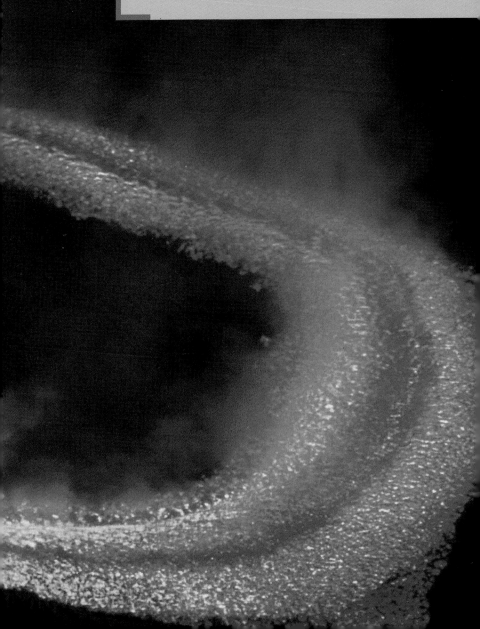

What causes volcanoes?

*There have always been volcanoes on our planet.
They act as vents, letting out the heat that is continuously
produced at the Earth's core.*

An opening leading to the bowels of the Earth

The Earth is like a blast furnace. As the radioactive elements in its rocks decay, they generate so much heat that the temperature of the Earth's core is over 5,000°C. Here and there in the upper mantle, at a depth of about 100km, the rocks melt to form magma. Volcanoes erupt when magma rises to the surface. However, some volcanoes provide outlets for material that originates at a much greater depth, thousands of kilometres from the surface.

Because magma is lighter and hotter than the surrounding rocks, it tends to rise towards the surface, pushing through weak areas in the Earth's crust and accumulating in vast reservoirs called magma chambers. As the magma rises and the pressure becomes less, the gases dissolved in the magma come out of solution and expand rapidly and explosively. The volcano erupts, and a mixture of gas, solid rock and melted rock bursts out.

> **GLOSSARY**
>
> **[Magma]**
> Liquid formed within the Earth through the melting of the materials from which the planet is made.
> **[Lithosphere]**
> Outermost layer of the Earth's structure, comprising the crust and the topmost part of the upper mantle.

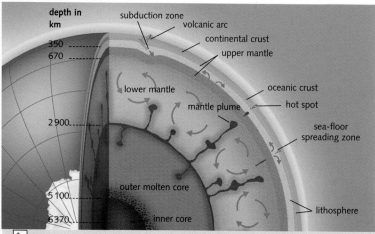

The Earth's mantle consists of hot rocks which have the ability to flow, moving the lithospheric plates above them. These convection movements allow the heat produced at the centre of the Earth to circulate and escape.

Plate tectonics

Volcanoes are mainly found around the edges of plates. The rigid outer layer of the Earth, the lithosphere, is divided into plates which move very slowly as a result of convection movements in the outer mantle. Some plates are made of lighter continental crust, others of dense oceanic crust. When two plates collide, the denser material slides under the lighter, which is then pushed upwards. The plate moving down heats up as it goes deeper and eventually melts into magma, which then moves upward. The point where this occurs is called a

Volcanic activity in Iceland results from the separation of two lithospheric plates. Here we see the rift structure that runs through the landscape of Pingvellir.

subduction zone. In these zones the lithosphere is destroyed. It is created along the mid ocean ridges, where two plates are being pulled apart, allowing material from the upper mantle to melt and rise to the surface, forming volcanoes which erupt basaltic lava flows. Plates may also simply slide along against each other. This does not generally lead to the creation of volcanoes.

Hot spot volcanoes

Around five per cent of volcanoes, known as hot spot volcanoes, appear in the middle of lithospheric plates. These are outlets for material originating at depths of nearly 3,000km, where the Earth's mantle meets its core. At this point the overheated material decompresses as it passes through the mantle and becomes liquefied. The resulting plume attacks the lithosphere like a blowtorch and ultimately perforates it, so that the volcano becomes active and magma can reach the surface.

The lithosphere continues to move while the plume remains still, which means that after a while the volcano is no longer located directly above the plume. When this happens the volcano becomes extinct, and a new one appears directly above the hot spot.

> **Map** (following pages)
>
> Most volcanoes appear along the edges of lithospheric plates. Volcanic chains form where new oceanic crust is being formed at the mid ocean ridges (spreading ridges), or in areas where plates converge and one sinks beneath the other (subduction zones). Only hot spot volcanoes appear outside these zones.

Active planet

Today it is estimated that the Earth has between 500 and 1,500 'active' volcanoes, or volcanoes that are liable to erupt at any time. During the 20th century, over 400 different volcanoes have erupted at least once. These figures need to be seen in context, as it is often hard to identify where each volcanic centre begins and ends, and the same centre may have several erupting cones. Moreover, the statistics do not include the tens of thousands of unknown volcanoes along rifts on the sea bed.

The volcanic zones

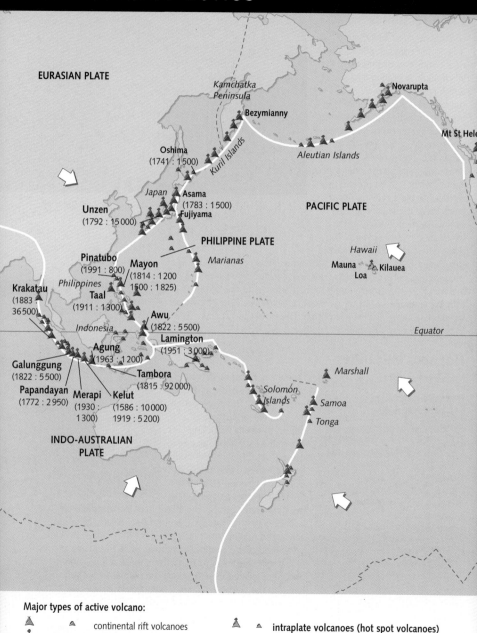

EURASIAN PLATE

Kamchatka
Peninsula

Novarupta

Bezymianny

Mt St Hele

Oshima
(1741 : 1500)

Kuril Islands

Aleutian Islands

Japan   Asama
         (1783 : 1500)

PACIFIC PLATE

Unzen
(1792 : 15000)   Fujiyama

PHILIPPINE PLATE

Hawaii

Pinatubo
(1991 : 800)   Mayon   Marianas
               (1814 : 1200   Mauna   Kilauea
Philippines   1500 : 1825)   Loa

Krakatau   Taal
(1883   (1911 : 1300)
36500)
               Awu
      Indonesia (1822 : 5500)   Equator
               Lamington
Agung   (1951 : 3000)

Galunggung   (1963 : 1200)
(1822 : 5500)   Marshall
               Tambora
Papandayan   (1815 : 92000)   Solomon
(1772 : 2950) Merapi Kelut   Islands   Samoa
               (1930 : (1586 : 10000)
               1300)   1919 : 5200)   Tonga

INDO-AUSTRALIAN
PLATE

Major types of active volcano:

continental rift volcanoes		intraplate volcanoes (hot spot volcanoes)	
oceanic rift volcanoes			
subduction zone volcanoes		inactive volcanoes	

very active active

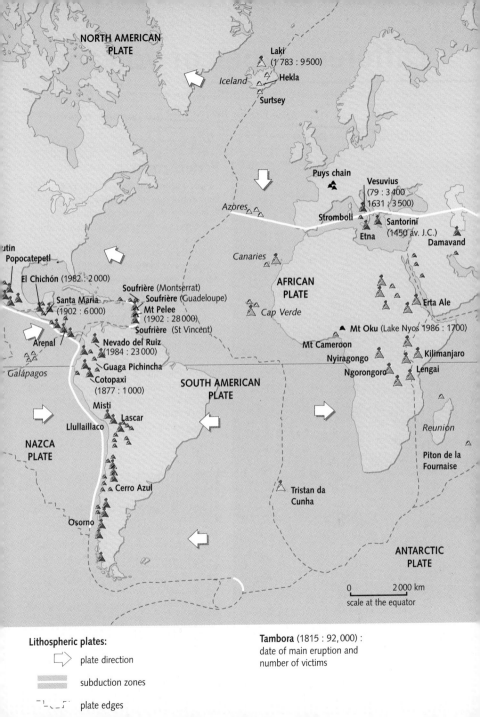

NORTH AMERICAN PLATE

Laki
(1 783 : 9 500)

Iceland

Hekla

Surtsey

Puys chain

Vesuvius
(79 : 3 400
1631 : 3 500)

Azores

Stromboli

Santorini
(1450 av. J.C.)

Etna

Damavand

AFRICAN PLATE

Canaries

Cap Verde

Erta Ale

...utin
Popocatepetl

El Chichón (1982 : 2 000)

Santa Maria
(1902 : 6 000)

Soufrière (Montserrat)

Soufrière (Guadeloupe)

Mt Pelee
(1902 : 28 000)

Soufrière (St Vincent)

Mt Oku (Lake Nyos 1986 : 1700)

Arenal

Nevado del Ruiz
(1984 : 23 000)

Mt Cameroon

Nyiragongo

Kilimanjaro

Galápagos

Guaga Pichincha

Cotopaxi
(1877 : 1 000)

SOUTH AMERICAN PLATE

Ngorongoro

Lengai

Misti

Lascar

Llullaillaco

Reunion

NAZCA PLATE

Cerro Azul

Tristan da Cunha

Piton de la Fournaise

Osorno

ANTARCTIC PLATE

0   2 000 km

scale at the equator

Lithospheric plates:

plate direction

subduction zones

plate edges

Tambora (1815 : 92,000) :
date of main eruption and
number of victims

Different types of volcano

Many volcanoes look like mountains with a crater at the summit. However, they may take other, more unusual shapes, forming calderas, faults or dome-like structures.

At 5,920m, the magnificent cone of the Llilicancabur volcano towers above Chile and the Bolivian Altiplano.

Perfect cones

Each volcano has its own history of events, comprising one or several eruptions, explosions of material or viscous flows. Each event gives a different appearance to the volcano.

The classic volcanic shape is the cone. Volcanoes of this type come in a great many different sizes (the smallest may rise to no more than a few metres), with comparatively steep slopes (around 30°). Mayon in the Philippines is famous for being the world's most regularly shaped volcano. Above a certain height volcanoes often have a snow-covered peak, like Fujiyama (3,776m), the highest mountain in Japan. Many volcanoes consist of several 'adventive' cones, each of which is a mini-volcano with a history of multiple eruptions (Etna has over 250 of these).

A temporary island

On 18 July 1831 a new island appeared in the Strait of Messina between Sicily and the Italian mainland. This was an underwater volcano that had risen high enough to reach the sea's surface. A month later the volcano had a diameter of 1,500m and a height of 70m. Many countries laid claim to the new land, but by the end of the year the island had disappeared, eroded by marine currents. After reappearing briefly in 1863, it sank, never to be seen again.

The summit of shield volcanoes seems almost flat. Mauna Ulu, formed between 1969 and 1974 on the slopes of Kilauea, offers a view of Mauna Loa, which rises to a height of 4,710m.

Shield volcanoes

Another type of volcano is much less obvious than the cone-shaped one. Shaped like a rugby ball half buried in the ground, the shield volcano has a slope of between 2° and 10°. Its characteristic convex shape results from pressure exerted by the liquid magma within, which makes its sides swell up before the magma slowly rises towards the surface. Shield volcanoes can reach a considerable height due to the accumulation of a vast quantity of magmatic material. The best-known shield volcano, Mauna Loa (in the volcanic archipelago of the Hawaiian Islands), also has the greatest volume of any volcano on Earth, rising to a height of 4,170m and with a base diameter of 250km.

GLOSSARY

[Spreading ridge]
An underwater fracture through which magma is forced, becoming part of the ocean floor.
[Rift valley]
Valley where the Earth's crust has collapsed due to extension of the lithosphere.

Large troughs

The ocean spreading ridges, Iceland and the Great African Rift Valley all show concentrations of volcanic phenomena. The magma flows up through the faults created as the lithospheric plates move apart, and fills them in. This gives rise to volcanoes of a very particular shape. When the plates move apart in a continent, a rift valley is created. The Great African Rift Valley is one example of such an effect. After a while this rift starts to transform into a sea, such as the Red Sea. Along the ocean spreading ridges on the sea floor, a large number of chimneys emit water laden with metallic salts. These are called black smokers.

Bumps and hollows

Volcanoes also have differently shaped summits. The classic shape is a crater; in other words, the vent is open at the top. The movements of the Earth's crust and the magma under the volcano often pull the crater in different directions, modifying its shape and depth.

If another eruption occurs in the same location, craters sometimes form within other craters. Depending on how active the volcano is, the bottom of the crater may be filled with solidified or boiling lava.

Sometimes, when the erupting magma meets surface water percolating through the volcanic rocks, the shock of the extreme contrast in temperatures leads to a great explosion of steam. A depression is then formed, in which a new lake may form. This type of crater is called a 'maar'.

Many volcanoes do not have a crater at all. If, at the end of an eruption, the mouth of the volcano fills with lava that is too viscous to flow out, the crater blocks up and the lava forms a dome. Mount St Helens in the United States and the Mont-Dore mountains in France are examples of this type.

labels: crater; accumulated layers of lava; adventive cone; eruptive fissure; magma chamber

Volcanoes are shaped by lava flows and the layers of volcanic ash that are ejected (pyroclastics). These create a more or less steep-sided cone around the main vent, which may be linked to one or more magma chambers.

GLOSSARY

[Caldera]
The summit of a volcano which has collapsed due to a particularly violent eruption and the emptying of the underlying magma chamber.
[Maar]
The crater formed when rising magma hits water.

The centre of the caldera of this Ethiopian volcano is partially filled with rainwater.

Devil's cauldrons: calderas

Calderas are large areas at the centre of some volcanic mechanisms, where the ground has collapsed. They occur during a particularly violent eruption, when the magma reservoirs beneath the volcano are suddenly emptied. A plain several kilometres across then forms at the centre of the volcano, cut off from the rest of the world by a ring of high cliffs.

Calderas can produce a range of landscapes. In Santorini, to the north of Crete, the collapse of the caldera in the centre of the island following an extremely violent eruption around 1500 BC has left no land at all apart from a steep, crescent-shaped cliff. The Ngorongoro caldera (Tanzania) has retained an extremely diverse range of animal life within a walled plain 20km in diameter. The area has been a world heritage site since 1979.

The largest caldera in the world (30km x 100km) is in Indonesia and contains Lake Toba.

Variable shape

The characteristics of volcanoes change over time. For example, a dome may be blown away by an eruption that literally cuts the volcano's head off. The largest eruption in recent history (1815) reduced the height of the volcano Tambora (Indonesia) from 4,000m to 2,800m. Other sudden changes can also occur: a lake may empty, or an island may suddenly appear in the middle of the ocean. Lastly, the effects of erosion and time may transform a sleeping volcano into a green and pleasant mountain. It was for this reason that the mountains of the Auvergne in France were not recognized as volcanic until the 18th century.

Different types of eruption

Plumes of volcanic ash from grey volcanoes and lava flows from red volcanoes are indicative of two different types of eruption. These differences depend largely on the composition of the rising magma.

The basic scenario

An eruption can be compared to the explosion of a champagne cork after the bottle has been shaken. The Earth's crust gives way under the pressure generated when the gas dissolved in the magma begins to come out of solution as the magma, which has accumulated in the magma chamber beneath the volcano, rises and the pressure decreases. The eruption takes place as bubbles of gas (water vapour, carbon dioxide, chlorine and other gases) suddenly expand, causing an explosion in which the partially solidified liquid is projected out of the volcano.

The form this expulsion takes depends on the gas and silica content of the magma. The more gas there is in the magma, the more violent the explosion. If the molten rock contains a lot of silica (over 70%), it will be more viscous and will not flow easily. It may even form blockages, which will eventually explode, projecting volcanic bombs and other highly dangerous rock debris. Conversely, if there is not much silica in the rock (less than 50%), it will flow in liquid streams of basaltic lava, with fire fountaining where some gas is being released.

Classification

Generally speaking, there are four types of eruption. Hawaiian eruptions do not involve many explosions and are characterized by flows of very hot, liquid lava. They create shield volcanoes. The presence of viscous, gas-rich magma means that Strombolian eruptions alternate between explosive emissions of pyroclastics and lava flows (the resulting cone is composed of a series of layers of pyroclastics and cooled lava). These volcanoes are called

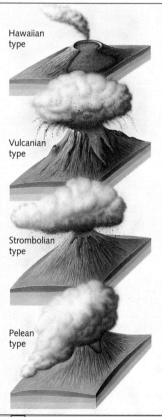

Hawaiian type

Vulcanian type

Strombolian type

Pelean type

There are four main categories of eruption, classified by the structure of the volcano and the chemical composition of the magma.

When lava meets shallow water large explosions are caused, as here in Iceland, near Surtsey.

stratovolcanoes. Vulcanian eruptions are among the most feared of all. In these cases the very viscous magma gets stuck on its way out of the volcanic vent, forming a blockage. When the accumulation of pressure in the vent reaches a certain point, this blockage explodes, ejecting a rain of pyroclastics over the surrounding area. Such eruptions can be recognized by the mushroom cloud of ash that is produced. Pelean eruptions are also explosive eruptions resulting from particularly viscous magma. They are characterized by the formation of a dome of cooled magma at the top of the vent. When this gives way, a high-temperature mass of volcanic ash and gas, known as a *nuée ardente*, pours down the sides of the volcano at a speed of several hundred kilometres an hour.

GLOSSARY

[Pyroclastics]
Projected debris emitted by a volcano, including dust, ash (2mm in diameter), lapilli (2–64mm) and bombs or blocks (more than 64mm).

Fire and water

When magma meets water other types of eruption occur. On the deep ocean floor, the enormous pressure of water prevents any release of gas, so the lava flows out without explosions. Such flows form pillow-like structures as they erupt and are known as 'pillow lavas'. In contrast, in shallower waters the contact between lava and water produces large explosions, known as phreatomagmatic eruptions. Lastly, movement of ground water in proximity to a magma chamber can cause the water to react with the hot rocks, forcing steam and solid rock to the surface. This is called a phreatic eruption.

Theoretical classification

Volcanoes are hard to classify. Often the same volcano experiences several types of eruption during its life (or even in the course of a single eruption). Piton de la Fournaise had eruptions of the Strombolian type, which were then superseded by the Hawaiian type.

A Fiery Earth **19**

Other dangers from volcanoes

Volcanoes represent a permanent threat of death to thousands of people on Earth. This threat can take many different forms, from toxic gas to mudslides.

Water-borne devastation

The disaster that struck the Colombian village of Armero on 13 November 1985 was a tragic reminder to the whole world that hot lava is not the only danger during a volcanic eruption. Like many other volcanoes, Nevado del Ruiz, rising to a height of 5,389m, is covered in glaciers. The heat of the eruption melted the ice, producing torrents of mud and water, which buried the town and its inhabitants. Twenty-two thousand people either died or disappeared.

Other types of volcano, such as those with craters containing lakes, can cause mudflows. This was how the former capital of Guatemala, Antigua, was destroyed in the 17th century. In hot, humid regions, mudflows may also appear during the rainy season in the years after an eruption that has left large deposits of ash. In Japan, one of the world's most advanced countries when it comes to preventing volcanic disasters, the slopes of Mount Usu were covered in ash by the eruptions of 1977–8. Dams and various filtration systems have since been built on the sides of the mountain, with the aim of controlling any mudflows that might pour down them. Particularly violent eruptions can also cause

The town of **Armero** (Colombia), 130km from Bogota, was buried by mudflows after the eruption of the volcano Nevado del Ruiz, which had been dormant since 1840.

devastating tidal waves. In 1883, the eruption that destroyed the island of Krakatau hurled so much material into the water that the coastlines of Java and Sumatra were swept by an enormous tidal wave, destroying 165 villages and killing 36,000 people.

Lethal gas

Volcanic craters sometimes fill with rainwater, forming lakes. Gases from the underlying magma such as sulphur dioxide, carbon dioxide and chlorine are continually being dissolved into the water. Kawah Ijen in Indonesia contains a lake filled with sulphuric and hydrochloric acid. Apart from the

The gas cloud released by Lake Nyos (Cameroon) on 21 August 1986 decimated animal herds in the vicinity. More than 3,000 cattle were recorded as having been asphyxiated by carbon dioxide.

intrinsic danger represented by the presence of such a vast quantity of acid, these crater lakes can suddenly give off large amounts of toxic gas. When the gases reach saturation point, the slightest instability can cause a massive release. In 1976, an enormous bubble of sulphur dioxide burst from the surface of Kawah Ijen's lake, killing 11 workers who were collecting sulphur. On 21 August 1986, there was a release of carbon dioxide from Lake Nyos in Mount Oku, an extinct volcano in north-western Cameroon, suffocating 1,746 people and 3,000 cattle.

Climate change

The release of large quantities of volcanic dust into the atmosphere can have consequences for the global climate. In 1982, the eruption of the El Chichón volcano in Mexico sent 20 million tonnes of dust and enormous quantities of sulphur dioxide into the stratosphere. The cloud is thought to have blocked 2–3% of sunlight for three years, leading to a planet-wide drop in temperatures of around 1°C. It was responsible for the breaking of cold-weather records in the USA during the winter of 1983–4 and in Europe the following year.

Planes under threat

In June 1982, a British Airways jumbo jet was flying over Java at an altitude of 12,300m when tonnes of volcanic dust, sent into the upper atmosphere by the eruption of Mount Galunggung, caused its engines to fail. Fortunately, the plane was able to make an emergency landing and no one on board was hurt.

Great eruptions of history

Many eruptions have left their mark on human history due to their power and devastating effects. Some have become legendary.

Santorini, the lost Atlantis?

In the year 1450 BC, one of the most destructive eruptions in history shook the island of Thira (now Santorini), to the north of Crete. Vulcanologists estimate that 60km^3 of material erupted into the atmosphere. The shock wave, heard thousands of kilometres away, demolished buildings in Greece, while a tidal wave flooded the surrounding coastlines. Most of the island collapsed into the sea. According to a Greek seismologist, this could have been the real origin of the legendary Atlantis. An Egyptian legend tells the story of a particularly advanced island civilization which suddenly disappeared after an earthquake and tidal wave.

In Santorini (Greece) the centre of the volcano collapsed, creating a partially submerged caldera. Here we see the crater and, behind it, the caldera cliff with the town of Phira at the top.

Pompeii falls victim to Vesuvius

Pompeii in Italy offers the most striking evidence of the destruction wreaked by volcanoes. In AD 79, Vesuvius erupted, burying the surrounding area in a deposit of ash, pumice and mud several metres thick. In the wealthy city of Pompeii, the ash preserved moulds of the bodies of those who were caught before they could flee. The eruption was described in detail by Pliny the Younger, the writer and Roman consul, who gave his name to the plume of pyroclastics thrown up during explosive eruptions: this is called a 'Plinian column'.

Krakatau, Montagne Pelée, Pinatubo

'Krakatau' is said to be the sound made by this Indonesian volcano when it is angry. On 27 and 28 August 1883 its rage was heard more than 4,500km away. The shock waves of the explosions shattered windows within a radius of 500km. The volcanic cloud rose 40km into

GLOSSARY

[Pumice]
Very light, porous volcanic rock.

During the eruption of Pinatubo (Philippines) in 1991, the sky was obscured by debris for months. The surrounding area was covered in a cloak of volcanic ash 1–10cm thick. Ash was even found as far afield as the coast of China.

the air and went several times round the Earth. Enormous quantities of pumice falling into the sea created devastating tidal waves, which were the main cause of the 36,000 human deaths recorded.

The eruption of the Montagne Pelée in Martinique marked a turning point in the history of vulcanology. This volcano, which had long been dormant, rose to 1,397m and contained a lake, formerly a favourite bathing spot for the inhabitants of the island's largest town, Saint-Pierre, located below the volcano. On 8 May 1902, the mountain exploded. A cloud of gas and burning ash descended on Saint-Pierre at a speed of around 160kph, destroying the town in a few minutes. Only two of the 30,000 inhabitants survived, one of them a prisoner who had been locked in a cell with thick walls. The event caught scientists by surprise. They came to the site of the disaster in large numbers, leading to the first major scientific study of an eruption.

The disaster of Pinatubo (Philippines) in 1991 confirmed that major eruptions often occur in volcanoes that have long been dormant. Fortunately, this eruption took two months to reach its peak, making it possible to evacuate 200,000 people from the danger zone. On 15 June a plume 40km high dropped ash and pumice across the entire region. This was followed by a typhoon (Yunya), causing devastating slides of mud and ash. In spite of the precautions that had been taken, the eruption of Pinatubo killed more than 800 people.

Volcano records

Highest extinct volcano: Nevado Ojos del Saldado (Chile), 6,863m. Highest active volcano: Antonfalla (Argentina), 6,450m. Largest active volcano: Mauna Loa (Hawaii), 40,000km³. Most deadly eruption: Tambora (Indonesia), 92,000 killed in 1815. Largest explosion ever known: Toba (Sumatra), 75,000 years ago.

Volcanoes and people

> Volcanoes arouse both fear and fascination. Today we try to control their energy, but still they take their toll in human lives.

Fertile but dangerous

Despite the risks involved, hundreds of thousands of people live beneath volcanoes. The land there is particularly fertile, due to the presence of ash rich in potassium, phosphorous and calcium. Java, a volcanic island in the Indonesian archipelago, contains 35 craters and has a population density of 880 per square kilometre. In a good year, three rice crops can be grown there. The land around Italy's Mount Etna is among the most fertile of the Mediterranean basin, producing large harvests of lemons and oranges every winter. The population density in the area is at record levels, with 500,000 people living in the vicinity of the volcano.

At the foot of the volcano Merapi (Indonesia), tobacco crops grow on land fertilized by mineral-rich volcanic debris.

Metals and precious stones

Volcanoes produce a great quantity of useful or highly valuable raw materials. For example, pumice stone, formed from solidified lava, is a porous rock with abrasive qualities. More generally, chemists are becoming increasingly interested in minerals of volcanic origin known as zeolites, due to their ability to accelerate reactions. In particular they are used in anti-pollution devices (in car exhausts, for example) to break down toxic molecules.

Volcanic sulphur also figures among the raw materials that are useful to the chemical industry. It is found in particular around Kawah Ijen in Indonesia, and in the world's highest sulphur mine around Purico in Chile.

Volcanic processes also concentrate the metals present in veins or seams in the Earth's mantle (copper, gold, silver and mercury). The eroded volcanoes of the Cascades chain in the western USA gave rise to the famous Gold Rush. The high levels of pressure in volcanoes also promote the crystallization of gemstones such as topaz, amethyst and

Icelanders like to meet and bathe in the natural hot springs to be found all over the island.

moonstones, while diamonds, which are created under high pressure at depths of almost 3,000km, may be brought to the surface by volcanic processes.

Controlling the energy of volcanoes

In volcanic regions, springs are sometimes heated up by the close proximity of magma, sometimes to over 300°C. When the temperature rises above 100°C the resulting steam can be used to drive power station turbines to produce electricity. The USA is the world's largest producer of geothermal electricity, followed by the Philippines and Italy. At lower temperatures the water is used directly for heating. Eighty per cent of Iceland's population use geothermal heating. The country even uses this cheap energy to grow tropical fruit in greenhouses.

Scientists are currently researching and developing mechanisms for harnessing the energy of volcanoes directly, without recourse to hot-water springs.

Thermal springs in Budapest

Geothermal heat produces hot springs almost everywhere in the world. In Budapest, for example, baths were built in the 1st century AD to help the Roman legions of Pannonia get back to full health. The city still has many thermal bathhouses, including one of the largest in Europe.

GLOSSARY

[Fumarolic gas]
Gaseous emissions from a volcano.
[Geothermal]
This refers to heat produced within the structure of the Earth.

The Earth is a living planet. Its solid surface is continually being renewed and reshaped by volcanic forces driven by convection within Earth's mantle. The thin rigid surface is also subjected to phenomenal tensions. These tensions accumulate over decades until they are released, causing the solid rock to fracture, producing earthquakes. When earthquakes occur under the ocean they can in turn cause tsunami that devastate the coastlines.

The earthquake that shook Japan in 1995 left 6,000 dead. This happened in a country which is well prepared for earthquakes and so underlines just how hard it is to manage the risks.

When the Earth moves

The causes of earthquakes

The Earth's crust is always imperceptibly changing under the influence of colossal forces. Surface rocks are distorted and break, causing destructive earthquakes.

Non-stop earthquakes

An earthquake is a movement of the Earth's crust which causes shaking at ground level, resulting in varying degrees of destruction. This movement may be due to an eruption, an underground explosion or the impact of a meteorite, but most often it is caused by a break in the rock lower down. A break of this kind is known as the 'focus' of the earthquake and, in 95% of cases, will be located in the brittle part of the lithosphere, less than 60km from the surface.

The planet is continually shaken by earthquakes, but most go unnoticed as they are very weak or affect uninhabited areas. Every year an average of one or two very large earthquakes (registering over 8 on the Richter scale), around a hundred medium earthquakes (over 6) and 100,000 small earthquakes (over 3) are recorded. Earthquakes can cause major damage (collapsed buildings, tsunami, avalanches and landslides), which in itself can claim a great many victims. In the last 100 years earthquakes have caused the deaths of more than 1.5 million people.

When the plates crack

According to the theory of tectonic plates, the brittle part of the Earth's crust (the lithosphere) is split into a dozen main plates, which move over a lower layer called the asthenosphere where the rocks, though solid, can flow under the high pressures. The junction between two plates is a particularly sensitive area. If the two plates move apart, as happens along spreading ridges in the ocean, molten rock from the mantle breaks through to form new oceanic crust. If the plates move together, the denser one sinks under the other and begins to melt at depths, while the lighter plate is raised up to form a mountain chain. The two plates may also slide along each other, creating what are called transform faults. These three possibilities impose very severe tensions within the rigid surface rocks, which stretch and distort like elastic until they reach breaking

Magnitude and intensity

Magnitude is a measure of the energy released by an earthquake, described in terms of the Richter scale, which is a logarithmic progression. This means that, in moving from one unit to the next up the scale, the quantity of energy is multiplied by 10. Thus, while an earthquake of magnitude 5 releases as much energy as a bomb of the type that was dropped on Hiroshima, magnitude 6 is equivalent to 10 bombs (the largest earthquake ever recorded, in Chile in 1960, reached a magnitude of 9.5). The intensity of an earthquake is the measure of its effects (from imperceptible trembling to the collapse of entire buildings), which depend largely on the firmness of the ground and the distance from the focus. The best-known scale for this is the Mercalli scale.

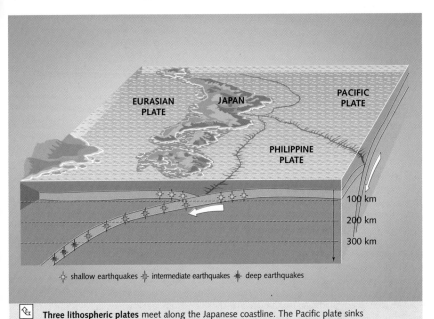

EURASIAN PLATE

JAPAN

PACIFIC PLATE

PHILIPPINE PLATE

100 km

200 km

300 km

✧ shallow earthquakes ✧ intermediate earthquakes ✧ deep earthquakes

Three lithospheric plates meet along the Japanese coastline. The Pacific plate sinks under the Philippine plate, which itself sinks under the Eurasian plate, which is a lighter, continental plate. Earthquakes fall into different categories according to the depth of their focus.

point, when they split along one or more fault lines. At this point the ground begins to shake.

Earthquakes may also occur away from the edge of any plate. This is often due to an old fracture which moves as a result of the forces exerted on the plate. Such earthquakes are usually, but not always, of low magnitude.

High-energy shock

When a fracture occurs in the Earth's crust, the energy of the shock is dispersed in the form of heat and 20–30% in the form of vibrations. Some of these waves (the most destructive) travel along the planet's surface, others travel through the crust. By measuring these waves it is possible to discover the distance from the focus and to find its location.

GLOSSARY

[Focus]
Point where the Earth movement takes place.

[Epicentre]
Closest point on the surface to the focus of the volcano.

[Macroseismic epicentre]
Place where the greatest intensity of an earthquake is felt.

Map (following pages)

The simplified plate tectonic model of the Earth's crust can be seen as a mosaic of moving plates. There are a dozen main plates, which create phenomenal tensions when they come into contact with each other (leading to faults and folds, and the stretching, thickening and thinning of the Earth's crust). This gives rise to the various kinds of earthquake.

Earthquake zones

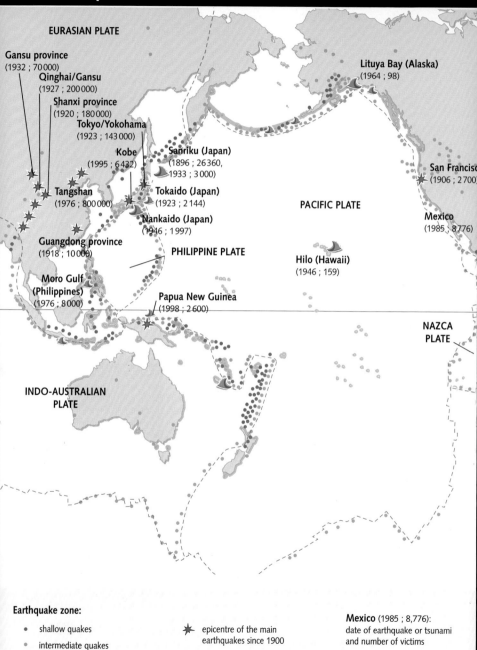

EURASIAN PLATE

Gansu province
(1932 ; 70 000)

Qinghai/Gansu
(1927 ; 200 000)

Shanxi province
(1920 ; 180 000)

Tokyo/Yokohama
(1923 ; 143 000)

Kobe
(1995 ; 6 432)

Sanriku (Japan)
(1896 ; 26 360,
1933 ; 3 000)

Tangshan
(1976 ; 800 000)

Tokaido (Japan)
(1923 ; 2 144)

Nankaido (Japan)
(1946 ; 1 997)

Guangdong province
(1918 ; 10 000)

PHILIPPINE PLATE

Moro Gulf
(Philippines)
(1976 ; 8 000)

Papua New Guinea
(1998 ; 2 600)

Lituya Bay (Alaska)
(1964 ; 98)

PACIFIC PLATE

San Francisco
(1906 ; 2 700)

Mexico
(1985 ; 8 776)

Hilo (Hawaii)
(1946 ; 159)

**NAZCA
PLATE**

**INDO-AUSTRALIAN
PLATE**

Earthquake zone:

- shallow quakes
- intermediate quakes
- deep quakes

★ epicentre of the main
earthquakes since 1900

Mexico (1985 ; 8,776):
date of earthquake or tsunami
and number of victims

NORTH AMERICAN
PLATE

Erzincan (Turkey) (1939 ; 32 700)
Spitak (Armenia) (1988 ; 25 000)
Rasht (Iran) (1988 ; 40 000)
Ashad (Turkmenistan)
(1948 ; 19 800)

central Italy
(1915 ; 35 000)

Tabas (Iran)
(1977 ; 15 000)

Avellino (Italy)
(1980 ; 12 383)

Karatag
(Tadjikistan)
(1907 ;
24 000)

Messina (Italy)
(1908 ; 65 000)

El Asnam (Algeria)
(1980 ; 16 000)

Izmit (Turkey)
(1999 ; 17 000)

Agadir (Morocco)
(1960 ; 13 100)

Jahrom (Iran)
(1972 ; 20 800)

Bhuj (India)
(2001 ; 20 000)

Quetta (Pakistan)
(1935 ; 30 000)

atemala
76 ; 23 000)

Kangra (India)
(1905 ; 29 000)

Equator

Aanagua (Nicaragua)
1972 ; 31 000)

AFRICAN PLATE

Yungay (Peru)
(1970 ; 54 000)

northern Chile
(1868 ; 25 674)

SOUTH AMERICAN
PLATE

tral Chile
50 ; 1260)

Chillan (Chile)
(1939 ; 28 000)

Tierra del Fuego (Argentina)
(1949 ; 10 000)

ANTARCTIC
PLATE

0   2 000 km

scale at the equator

Main tsunamis since 1890:

waves below 15m high

waves above 15m high

coastlines at risk from
tsunami

Great earthquakes of history

The historical record is punctuated by violent outbursts of the Earth's energy. Earthquakes and tsunami can affect almost any region on the planet.

Europe studies the problem

Empirical observations of earthquakes were rare in Europe before the 18th century. Before then, any explanations of the phenomena were based largely on the writings and theories of Aristotle and Pliny. In 1750, England was hit by five large earthquakes. On 1 November 1755, a cataclysmic shock caused a tsunami that hit the shores of Portugal, submerging Lisbon and killing 70,000 people. These two events mark the beginning of modern seismology. The first studies of the location, length and effects of earthquakes were made at this time, notably by John Michell of Great Britain and Elie Bertrand of Switzerland.

A street in Kobe, Japan's largest port, after the earthquake of 17 January 1995.

China takes precautions

The two most deadly disasters in history both took place in China. In 1556, an earthquake killed 830,000 people in Shanxi and Henan; in 1976, a similar number were killed in the Tangshan region. For thousands of years the Chinese have sought to protect themselves. An earthquake detector from the early 1st century AD has been found, in the form of a vase mounted with dragons holding a ball in their mouths. At the slightest tremor the ball falls. Today, in addition to many scientific stations, a network of volunteers monitors signs such as animal behaviour or changes in the levels of lakes and wells. In 1975, people were evacuated hours before an earthquake struck, saving thousands of lives.

San Francisco in ruins

At around 5am on 18 April 1906, San Francisco Bay was hit by violent shocks lasting between 45 and 60 seconds. At its height the earthquake was felt within a radius of around 500km, from southern Oregon to southern Los Angeles on the coast, and as far as central Nevada inland. A 470km-long crack opened near San Francisco, while in the city itself a fire broke out which raged for four days. Almost 3,000 people were killed across the region and 28,000 buildings were destroyed. The disaster marked a turning point in the study of earthquakes.

After the **earthquake** of 1906, the partially destroyed city of San Francisco was ravaged by fire.

Observations established a striking correlation between the scale of the damage and geological conditions underground. Buildings that had stood in a line before the catastrophe no longer did so after it. From his observations, Professor Harry Fielding Reid deduced that earthquakes are the result of tensions that have built up within the Earth's crust over a number of years.

Chile: the most powerful earthquake in history

In 1960, Chile suffered the most powerful earthquake known in history. The series of tremors began on 21 May and a 1,000km-long crack opened along the fault line. Worst of all, an enormous tsunami submerged the coastline of the Pacific Basin. In Chile, the earthquake left 1,500 dead and destroyed 60,000 houses. The tsunami caused 61 deaths in Hawaii, 200 in Japan and 32 in the Philippines. In Hawaii, blocks of rock were carried 180m inland. In Chile, the landscape underwent major modifications, with rockfalls and landslides creating a lake on the San José River. On 24 May, the volcano Puyhue began to erupt.

GLOSSARY

[Seismology]
The science of earthquakes.

India in shock

In January 2001, India was just starting its Republic Day celebrations when the entire subcontinent was shaken by an earthquake. The epicentre occured close to the border with Pakistan, in the north of the province of Gujarat. Trains were derailed, the city of Bhuj (population 150,000) was left in ruins and there were 20,000 dead across the region. The earthquake measured 7.7 on the Richter scale.

Tsunami:
tidal waves

> *When an earthquake occurs under the ocean, there is a high risk that enormous and exceptionally powerful waves will engulf the nearby coastlines. These waves are called tsunami.*

Deadly waves

The word 'tsunami' comes from the Japanese tsu ('harbour') and nami ('wave'). It refers to a wave – or series of waves – in a sea or lake which engulf a coastline, causing serious damage to people and property. Tsunami are caused by sudden disturbances that displace a large amount of water: earthquakes, landslides, debris from a volcanic eruption falling into the water, nuclear explosions and even meteorite impacts. Eighty per cent of tsunami occur in the Pacific Ocean.

GLOSSARY
[Refraction] Phenomenon in which a wave rolls in on itself, due to the different speeds of its various parts located at different heights.

Scenario for disaster

When a tsunami forms in the open sea, it goes more or less unnoticed. However, it quickly travels towards more sensitive areas, covering thousands of kilometres at a speed proportional to the depth of the water. In the Pacific, for example, where the water reaches depths of 5,000m, tsunami move at around 800kph, each separated from the next

In 1868, an earthquake shook the Chilean and Peruvian coastline, causing an enormous trans-Pacific tsunami which swept through the port of Arica (Chile).

Raising the alarm

Twenty-six states around the Pacific Ocean are involved in the Tsunami Warning System, whose centre, based near Honolulu, collects data from maritime and seismological stations throughout the Pacific Basin. As soon as the first indications of an earthquake are felt, it calculates and locates the risks of tsunami. Alerts are sent out to seafarers and populations living by affected coasts; the latter are then able to take refuge on higher ground.

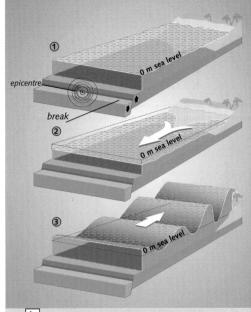

An earthquake causes the vertical displacement of a column of water. This disturbance is almost imperceptible in the open sea, but increases as it approaches the shore. The shallowness of the water combines with friction to create a gigantic wave.

by around 200km. As they reach the coastline they slow down, but their height simultaneously increases to 10m, 20m or even 30m. In Japan in 1771, an earthquake caused the highest tsunami ever recorded, at 84m. When it reaches the coast, refraction causes the tsunami to take on the characteristic shape of a breaking wave. The various parts of the wave are not subject to the same constraints; for example, the crest moves faster than the base, which is held back by friction and turbulence created by contact with the sea bed. This difference in speed causes the wave to fold back on itself. The sea suddenly pulls back at the shoreline, before returning in the form of a wall of water of unimaginable power. In 1883, the eruption of Krakatau in Indonesia caused a terrible tsunami. A warship at anchor nearby, the Berow, was found 3km inland and 9m above sea-level.

Imamura-Iida Intensity Scale

Magnitude	Wave height in open water	Wave height on the coast	Effects
0	up to 0.10 m	1 m	No damage
1	up to 0.25 m	2 m	Houses and ships in the coastal area affected
2	up to 0.50 m	4-6 m	Destruction of boats, possible fatalities
3	up to 1 m	10-20 m	Destruction along a 200m stretch of coastline
4	up to 2 m	30 m	Destruction along a 500m stretch of coastline

he air around us obeys the strict laws of physics. Its movement is determined by temperature – warm air rises but cold air falls. These convection movements, which are linked to the Earth's rotation, are the cause of winds. Winds are affected by a great many factors (such as the proximity of an ocean or mountains, or the tilt of the Earth), sometimes leading to violent events including gales, thunderstorms, tornadoes and cyclones. Today, computer simulations are helping us to improve our understanding of these events.

Hurricane George, which hit the Caribbean islands and the American coastline in September 1998, blew at a steady speed of 240kph, gusting to 305kph.

Wild winds

The causes of wind

A wind is caused by a temperature difference between two masses of air in the atmosphere. Its development is influenced by the movement of the planet and geographical features.

Moving air

When heat is applied to a gaseous mixture such as air, the molecules of nitrogen, oxygen and hydrogen start to move. Molecules collide more and more often, causing them to ricochet away from each other, with the result that the gaseous mixture loses density. A hot gas is lighter and less dense than a cold gas. This is the governing principle behind the phenomenon of wind.

When a mass of air is heated by the sun, or by some warm element in the environment, it gets lighter and rises. At high altitudes the air mass cools and sinks again. During

Depression in the northern hemisphere

northern hemisphere

southern hemisphere

isobar

geostrophic wind   A = anticyclone
surface wind   D = depression

Points where the pressure is the same are linked by lines known as isobars. In the northern hemisphere surface winds blow in a clockwise direction around an anticyclone, and in an anticlockwise direction around a depression. These directions are reversed in the southern hemisphere.

this time, the Earth has rotated slightly on its axis, so that the air mass will sink to a point further east if it is in the northern hemisphere, further west in the southern hemisphere.

At the point where the air was heated, a zone of low pressure (a depression) is created.

Föhn effect

When a mountain range stands in the way of a dominant wind, a 'Föhn effect' occurs. The air mass builds up on the mountainside and cools. The water vapour it carries condenses, resulting in showers. As it loses water, the air mass rises, crosses the mountain range and descends on the other side, where, with its increased pressure, it becomes far warmer than it was at the same altitude on the side where it first met the mountains.

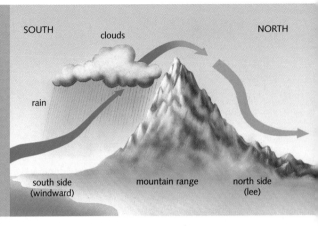

SOUTH   clouds   NORTH

rain

south side (windward)   mountain range   north side (lee)

Conversely, where the cold air sinks down, a zone of high pressure (an anticyclone) appears. As a fluid tends spontaneously to re-establish equal pressure in all its parts, so air masses move from anticyclones to depressions. These major principles underlie general movements in the air, but they are continually contradicted by a number of localized phenomena, whose effects are cumulative.

Sea wind

One of the main local disturbances stems from the different thermal behaviour of land and water. The ground rapidly changes temperature, whereas water has a greater thermal capacity, meaning that it takes longer to heat or cool. During the day, and more generally throughout the summer, the air masses over the oceans are cooler than those above the continents. As a result damp air moves from the ocean towards the land. This is the phenomenon underlying the African and Asian monsoons. The most striking illustration of this principle is the alternation between on-shore and off-shore breezes. During the day the on-shore breeze blows from the sea onto the land (where air heats up more quickly), while the off-shore breeze blows in the opposite direction at night, from the rapidly cooled land towards the sea.

Map *(following pages)*

While tropical cyclones travel from east to west, gales in the temperate zones generally move from west to east. They are very violent in the southern hemisphere between 35° and 70° latitude (the 'roaring forties' and 'furious fifties'). Tornadoes are localized; they often occur in the USA, but also affect other regions in the world.

Mountain maze

Mountains represent a major obstacle to moving masses of air. Depending on their original direction, winds may be diverted, greatly slowed or indeed accelerated if they blow through a narrow valley that creates a bottleneck. These specific conditions create local wind systems, some of which are highly complex.

Cyclones, storms and tornadoes

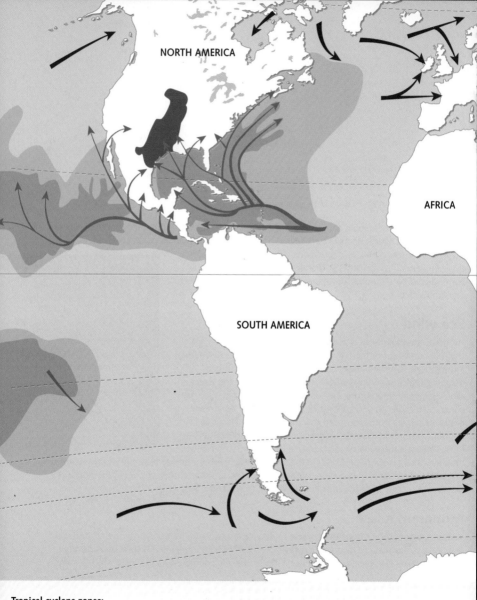

NORTH AMERICA

AFRICA

SOUTH AMERICA

Tropical cyclone zones:

moderate

strong or very strong

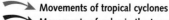 Movements of tropical cyclones

Movements of gales in the temperate zones

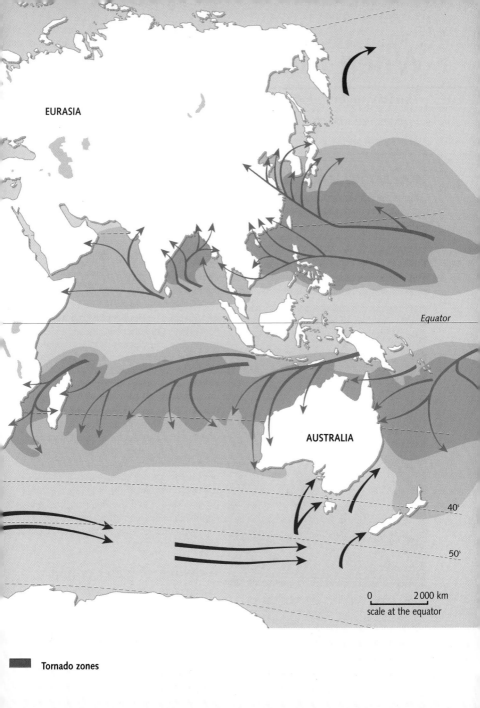

EURASIA

Equator

AUSTRALIA

40°

50°

0   2 000 km
scale at the equator

Tornado zones

When thunder roars

Thunder, lightning, torrential rain – storms produce impressive effects. They occur only if specific conditions are fulfilled.

How storms form

Storms generally occur at the end of a particularly hot day. At that time the ground releases water vapour, which rises into the atmosphere until it reaches colder regions, where it condenses. The water passes from a gaseous state to a liquid state, in the form of tiny droplets suspended in the air. A cloud appears. The droplets at the base of the cloud are warmer and lighter, so they tend to rise. The water vapour continues to condense. This change of state releases energy, which causes the rising movements to accelerate, sometimes to as much as 160kph. The cloud swells to become an enormous cumulonimbus, shaped like a giant tower. The many water droplets it contains block the sunlight and make it look very dark. The top of the cloud may reach an altitude of 8–15km. At this height the droplets in the cloud combine and sometimes freeze. They become heavier and fall back down through the cloud. Some of these droplets have an electrical charge probably acquired by collisions, with the smaller droplets positively charged and the larger ones holding a negative charge. This leads to the upper regions of the cloud having a net positive charge and the lower regions, a net negative charge. Lightning is an electrical discharge between the positive and negative regions of the thunder cloud.

High, electrically charged clouds are conducive to the passage of electricity between two parts of the same cloud, between two different clouds, or between a cloud and the ground.

A deluge of water or hail

Large drops of water accumulate at the top of the cloud and sometimes freeze. When they reach a critical weight, they drop back down through the cloud to fall as showers of rain or hail, which may be very violent. A

Cumulonimbus clouds can reach a height of 10km in the temperate zones and 16–17km in the intertropical region (pictured are clouds in Namibia).

storm often produces as much as 50 to 100 litres of water per square metre in a few hours. This precipitation causes the air temperature to drop, and the localized cooling causes wind speeds to increase. When a storm broke over the airport of Toulouse-Blagnac in France in 1989, the temperature dropped from 29°C to 16°C in six minutes and hailstones 3cm in diameter hammered on the tarmac, while the wind began to blow at over 140kph.

Devastating hailstones

In theory, water freezes at 0°C, but in practice it sometimes remains in an unstable, liquid state at much lower temperatures. This phenomenon, called 'supercooling', can be seen for example in storm clouds, in which the water droplets may have temperatures between 0°C and –15°C. When they come into contact with a small piece of ice, they also freeze and add to its mass. In this way hailstones may grow to a diameter of several centimetres. When they become too heavy they fall, encountering higher temperatures on the way and partially melting before they hit the ground.

Thunder – a time-bomb

Lightning is an electrical discharge, causing the air to heat up suddenly and intensely. This compresses the adjacent clear air and forms a shock wave, which spreads out from the lightning until it reaches our eardrums, causing them to vibrate, and we hear thunder. As sound waves travel more slowly than light, thunder claps reach us some time after we see the lightning that caused them.

The causes of cyclones

In late summer, contact between seawater that is still warm and the cooling atmosphere generates a colossal amount of energy, causing cyclones that may be highly destructive.

Portrait of a killer

A tropical cyclone is a whirling disturbance whose source lies somewhere in the zone between the tropic of Cancer and the tropic of Capricorn, excluding a 500km strip on either side of the equator. If the wind speed is less than 62kph it is called a 'tropical depression', becoming a 'tropical storm' at wind speeds of 62–117kph. The term 'hurricane' is reserved for particularly violent cyclones, with winds of over 117kph. About 50 hurricanes are identified annually, 70% of which affect the northern hemisphere. The most violent occur in the north-western Pacific. Hurricanes are characterized by a great cloudy mass with a radius of 500–1,000km, curling into a spiral around an eye which is 10–50km wide. Inside the eye of the storm the wind is light and pressure minimal. Around it the wind and precipitation reach violent levels.

Born at sea

Cyclones arise from the differing thermal behaviour of water and air. In late summer, when the ocean has soaked up the heat of the sun over a period of months, it reaches a temperature of over 26°C; meanwhile the air, reacting to changes in temperature much more quickly, is already cooling. The water vapour given off by the ocean therefore condenses quickly on contact with the air. Condensation is a chemical process which releases energy. It can supply a cyclone with more energy than the annual output of electricity in the USA. This energy heats the air, creating a zone of very low pressure near the surface of the ocean. The surrounding air pours into this depression to fill it. Air is also subject to the Coriolis force, caused by the Earth's rotation, which makes moving fluids veer to the right in the northern hemisphere and to the left in the

The three white spirals, each with a plainly visible eye, show the positions of Cyclone Andrew on 23, 24 and 25 August 1992 as it entered the Gulf of Mexico before reaching the Florida coast.

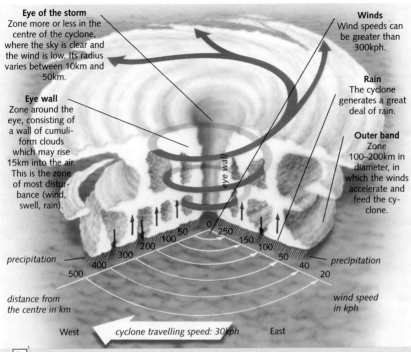

Eye of the storm
Zone more or less in the centre of the cyclone, where the sky is clear and the wind is low. Its radius varies between 10km and 50km.

Eye wall
Zone around the eye, consisting of a wall of cumuliform clouds which may rise 15km into the air. This is the zone of most disturbance (wind, swell, rain).

Winds
Wind speeds can be greater than 300kph.

Rain
The cyclone generates a great deal of rain.

Outer band
Zone 100–200km in diameter, in which the winds accelerate and feed the cyclone.

eye wall

precipitation 500 400 300 200 100 50 0 250 150 100 50 40 20 precipitation

distance from the centre in km

wind speed in kph

West   cyclone travelling speed: 30kph   East

Section of a cyclone. A cyclone generally travels from east to west at an average speed of around 30kph. As it passes it creates a deep area of low pressure, which may cause sea levels to rise by 3–8m.

southern hemisphere. The sinking movement due to the depression, combined with the Coriolis force, turns into a whirl. The winds and the Coriolis force then start to move the cyclone. The path it follows often takes the form of a parabola, but it may be atypical. Some hurricanes suddenly change direction, travel in loops or go back the way they came. The cyclone's intensity lessens once it leaves the ocean and travels over a continental zone, which explains why the damage it causes will often be restricted to an area within 200km of the coast.

Multiple effects

Hurricanes are accompanied by winds of over 120kph, which can uproot trees and flatten buildings. They may degenerate into localized tornadoes. The torrential rains that accompany them may also cause terrible landslides. However, the most deadly phenomenon associated with hurricanes is the storm tide. This is an abnormal rise in the sea level caused by the depression, which acts on the surface of the water like a huge sucker. A tide of this kind killed 300,000 people in Bangladesh in 1970 and 10,000 more in India in 1999.

Great cyclones of history

Some regions have an annual cyclone season. The most severe cyclones have hit the islands and coastal regions of the tropics.

The Bathurst Bay cyclone

On 4 March 1899, Cyclone Mahina hit the Australian coastline. Contemporary accounts describe an exceptional storm tide 14m high in Bathurst Bay. The huge wave engulfed 152 boats and more than 300 sailors. Ships and animals (including dolphins) were found several kilometres inland and at altitudes of several metres. Around 100 Aborigines living in the nearby forest were also killed.

Recurrent disasters in Bangladesh

Bangladesh is regularly assaulted by cyclones coming from the Bay of Bengal. The years 1971, 1977 and 1999 were particularly bad. However, the most destructive cyclone was that of 1970, in which somewhere between 300,000 and 1 million people died. The region, overpopulated due to its agricultural importance (rice paddies), was totally devastated. Coastal crops and infrastructure were swept away. This cyclone, and the war of independence that followed, added the newly created country of Bangladesh to the list of the world's poorest nations. In the early 1990s, with the help of Western organizations, the Bangladeshi government constructed a number of storm shelters.

Cyclone Andrew undoubtedly caused the most material damage in history. The cost of its passage through the Bahamas, Florida and Louisiana in 1992 was estimated at 30 billion dollars.

GLOSSARY

[Typhoon]
The name for cyclones in the Far East.

Between 1973 and 1997, Bangladesh suffered three storms, four floods, a tsunami and two cyclones. The total death toll was over 400,000, with a further 42,000 affected (above, after the cyclone and tidal wave of April 1991).

Hugo the terrible

On 9 September 1989, a harmless accumulation of cumulonimbus clouds left the African continent near Senegal. Two days later these clouds had caused a tropical depression, which passed to the south-east of Cape Verde and soon turned into a hurricane. It was given the name Hugo. This cyclone was one of the large family of Cape Verde cyclones caused by instability in the lower layer of the troposphere (called 'African easterly waves'), due to contrasting temperatures between the sub-Saharan heat and the cool Gulf of Guinea. The hurricane took seven days to cross the Atlantic, hitting Guadeloupe on 16 September. Although the island's meteorological station was destroyed, it was possible to take some measurements: the 220kph winds were estimated to have gusted up to 300kph, destroying all in their path. A cyclonic wave of 3m was recorded, which carried boats up to 2.5m above sea-level. The hurricane rapidly declined after hitting South Carolina on 22 September.

Record horrors

→ The most intense cyclone, in other words the one that generated the strongest winds ever recorded, was Typhoon Tip, with winds of up to 305kph (north-western Pacific Ocean, 12 October 1979). Tip is also regarded as the largest ever cyclone, with winds of over 60kph across a diameter of 2,200km.

→ Typhoon Forrest, which swept across the same zone in September 1983, holds the record for the fastest intensification. The strongest winds increased from 120kph to 285kph in 24 hours.

→ The highest ever storm tide, at 14m, was caused by the Bathurst Bay cyclone (Australia) in 1899.

→ Cyclone John, which developed in the southern basin of the Pacific Ocean in August and September 1994, was the longest-lived, at 31 days.

Storms

While the tropics have their cyclones, the temperate regions have storms, which break over the continent after passing through specific ocean corridors.

When hot meets cold

Storms are born of small disturbances generated along the border between two masses of air at different temperatures. Air masses are parcels of atmosphere at a relatively homogeneous temperature and pressure. A warm air mass contains more water vapour than a cold air mass and has lower pressure. Zones where there is a sudden transition between two air masses are called 'atmospheric fronts'. When one of these fronts is subject to disturbance, strong, whirling winds may result. At the same time the dampness in the warm mass condenses on contact with the cold front, causing precipitation. In late autumn there are great contrasts in temperature between the tropical air masses warmed by the ocean and the polar masses, which are already very cold. This contrast destabilizes the front and causes storms.

This coloured satellite image shows the large storm that formed above Kamchatka Peninsula in the Bering Strait, on 2 April 1978.

Running on tracks

Storms are born far from the zone in which they break. For example, the storms that hit Europe originate in disturbances arising around Newfoundland. They then cross the Atlantic in a few days, following a corridor running more or less along the 50th parallel. Corridors of this kind are called 'tracks' and function a bit like a travelator whose 9km-high motors are the jet streams, consisting of tubes of very strong wind that supply travelling

Storm of the century

During the afternoon of 15 October 1987, winds were light over most of the UK, but a depression was developing over the Bay of Biscay. This moved northwards, and by midnight it was over the English Channel. Early on 16 October, warnings of Force 11 gales were issued. The depression moved rapidly northeast, and dramatic temperature increases were associated with the passage of its warm front. The strongest gust recorded over the UK was 106 knots at Gorleston, Norfolk, and gusts of more than 90 knots were recorded at several other coastal locations. Even well inland, gusts exceeded 80 knots: 86 knots was recorded at Gatwick, where the authorities closed the airport. The devastation was significant, with 15 million trees lost. Falling trees and masonry damaged or destroyed buildings and cars. Numerous small boats were wrecked or blown away, and a ship capsized at Dover.

The storm killed 18 people in England and at least four more in France. The death toll might have been far greater had the storm struck in the daytime.

Violent storms can cause devastation of natural resources, such as forests, on a large scale.

depressions with energy so that they can move along and in some cases expand, before breaking over the continent of Europe. The tracks function a bit like a river bed. At the point where they begin, to the west, the wind accelerates like water in a confluence zone. Where they end, to the east, the stream fans out and its speed reduces.

Storms follow each other along these tracks at a rate of one per day in winter; however, most are lost at sea.

These relatively permanent tracks are modified by the depressions they carry. The Atlantic track may end over England, or continue on to Germany, or fork in two different directions. Because the track brings dampness into these regions, its position determines whether the various countries will have a mild, damp winter or a cold, dry one.

Tornadoes

Although tornadoes are small and created by localized instability, they can become very violent. Their size makes them almost impossible to predict.

Between heaven and earth

A tornado is a column of air that spins violently. It travels over the ground and is connected to a cloud. Usually this is a storm cloud, a cumulonimbus. The tornado draws its energy from the sharp contrast between the temperature, pressure and humidity of the cloud and that of the ground. This contrast causes air under high pressure to pour into low-pressure areas, spiralling as it does so. The resulting winds usually blow at less than 160kph, but in exceptional cases they may increase to more than 400kph.

Tornadoes differ from other phenomena of a similar kind in being highly localized and on a much smaller scale. They generally travel only a few kilometres along the ground and their diameter remains less than 100m. However, some exceptional tornadoes remain in contact with the ground over more than 80km and attain diameters of 1km.

Tornadoes are small phenomena that release the energy of the contrasting conditions
at ground level and in the atmosphere.

The causes of tornadoes

Several factors contribute to the formation of a tornado, including very damp ground, the arrival of a mass of dry air and an unstable atmosphere (that is, an atmosphere in which the temperature drops rapidly as altitude increases).

Warm, damp air is forced upwards when the cold, dry front arrives. It quickly gains height and starts to become saturated with water due to the drop in temperature. The water in the warm mass condenses to form a cloud loaded with droplets. Its rapid rise causes a sudden depression under the cloud, into which the winds rush, spiralling as they go. One or several tornadoes form between the cloud and the ground. They may be visible (as though made of smoke), or almost invisible, in which case they are noticeable only from the dust circles they cause on the ground.

Tornadoes may be connected to local storms. In this case they grow larger and last longer.

Hard to predict

Digital models used by meteorological programs are based on a comparatively large-scale grid of the territory (several kilometres per section). At such a scale tornadoes are invisible. Forecasters are reduced to monitoring the occurrence of conditions that might give rise to tornadoes. The Gulf of Mexico is a particularly sensitive zone. The ocean heats up the atmosphere, producing warm, damp air. In contrast the mountains and deserts of the interior produce very dry masses of air. When these two masses meet, a particular kind of front called a 'dryline' is formed, providing the right conditions for large tornadoes to develop.

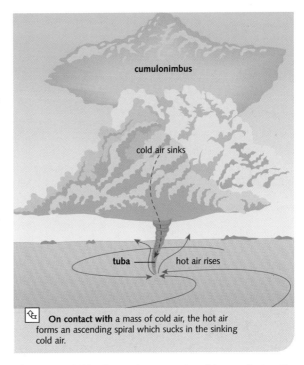

cumulonimbus

cold air sinks

tuba — hot air rises

On contact with a mass of cold air, the hot air forms an ascending spiral which sucks in the sinking cold air.

Sand devils

The hot, dry air above deserts gives rise to some odd sights. In the middle of the day, the dry air may be disturbed by a light breeze. This combination produces mini-tornadoes, spirals of dust and sand. These little tornadoes are not dangerous, as their winds seldom rise above 50kph; however, they make a big impression on the overheated minds of desert travellers.

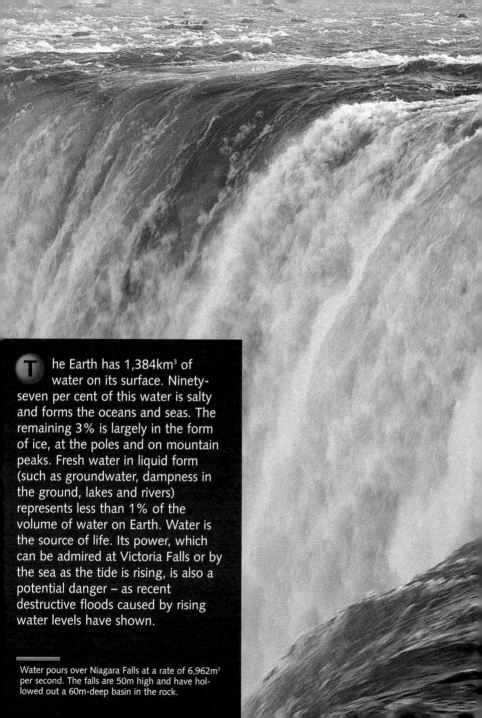

he Earth has 1,384km³ of water on its surface. Ninety-seven per cent of this water is salty and forms the oceans and seas. The remaining 3% is largely in the form of ice, at the poles and on mountain peaks. Fresh water in liquid form (such as groundwater, dampness in the ground, lakes and rivers) represents less than 1% of the volume of water on Earth. Water is the source of life. Its power, which can be admired at Victoria Falls or by the sea as the tide is rising, is also a potential danger – as recent destructive floods caused by rising water levels have shown.

Water pours over Niagara Falls at a rate of 6,962m³ per second. The falls are 50m high and have hollowed out a 60m-deep basin in the rock.

Raging waters

Rising water levels and floods

> *Most countries are regularly subject to flooding caused by sudden rises in water level. The phenomenon seems to be on the increase in temperate regions.*

A worldwide risk

Flooding is caused by rises in water levels and involves the submerging of an area of land, which may or may not be inhabited. During normal periods, the system of streams and rivers can cope with the volumes of water produced, retaining them within well-defined river channels. When abnormally high volumes of water are produced, the alluvial system may not cope with the volume of water within the channel system and flooding may result.

More than half of all natural disasters involve flooding, killing an average of 20,000 people throughout the world every year. The material damage caused is always very serious. Rising water levels and flooding affect most countries in the temperate zones and more or less every country in the tropical and subtropical zones. The most catastrophic flooding occurs in Asia, during the annual monsoon period. Dry air above the Himalayas creates a strong depression, which draws in damp air from the sea. When this air mass reaches the mountain

On **17 August 2002**, the historic city of Dresden in Germany found itself under water. Swollen by several days of continual rain, the Elbe stabilized at 9.40m.

range, it rises and condenses as it cools. The monsoon rains break, sometimes pouring more than 1,000mm of water a day onto the plain.

Water concentrates in catchment areas

Major rises in water level have a range of causes. The spring melt of snows in mountainous regions (nival regime), melting glaciers in a high-level basin (glacial regime) or heavy precipitation (pluvial regime, the most common) may all play a part.

The catchment area of a watercourse is the area within which all a river's tributaries join together to form a single river system.

At times of heavy precipitation, all the watercourses of the catchment area are in spate, bringing the rainwater to the main river, whose level also rises. The speed of the rise is influenced by the geography of the catchment area. Water will take much longer to become concentrated in a long, narrow basin than it does in a small, circular basin, where the rise will be very fast.

limit of surface water run-off
limit of groundwater run-off
outlet
impermeable layer (subsoil)

➡ surface water
➡ groundwater

The catchment area or hydrographic basin is the zone from which all the water flows into a single river system. The area where the surface water leaves the catchment area is called the outlet.

Zones liable to flooding

The rainwater that falls on a region does not necessarily cause the level of its main rivers to rise. Much of it goes back into the atmosphere through evaporation. A large amount sinks into the ground, where it joins the groundwater. It may surface again some distance away if the levels rise. The rest trickles down to end up in a river. The proportions falling into each category can vary considerably according to the amounts of precipitation, the temperature, and the shape and nature of the terrain.

More flooding?

Human activity is fundamentally changing the climate. Today, it is at least partially blamed for global warming, which itself may be a source of flooding in various ways: increases in rainfall, a rise in sea levels, changes to the vegetation which disturb the usual flow rates of rivers, and so on. In the temperate regions, scientists predict that a rise in temperature will lead to longer periods of drought, alternating with periods of flooding.

Map (following pages)

The largest river basins on the planet, formed by major rivers and all the tributaries of various sizes that feed into them, are located within large continents. Under certain geological conditions water may be held back in particular places, leading to the formation of lakes. Sudden changes in the terrain caused by a range of factors (earthquakes, volcanoes, glaciers, erosion) give rise to sometimes spectacular waterfalls and cataracts.

Rivers, lakes and waterfalls

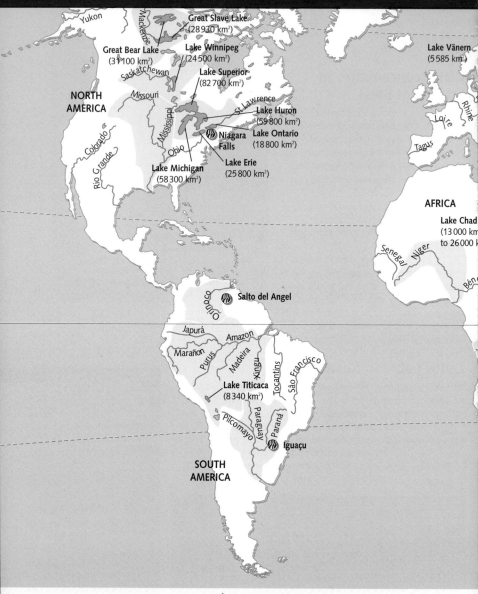

Yukon

Mackenzie

Great Slave Lake
(28 930 km²)

Great Bear Lake
(31 100 km²)

Lake Winnipeg
(24 500 km²)

Saskatchewan

Lake Superior
(82 700 km²)

**NORTH
AMERICA**

Missouri

St Lawrence

Lake Huron
(59 800 km²)

Mississippi

Colorado

Rio Grande

Ohio

Niagara
Falls

Lake Ontario
(18 800 km²)

Lake Michigan
(58 300 km²)

Lake Erie
(25 800 km²)

Lake Vänern
(5 585 km²)

Loire

Rhine

Tagus

AFRICA

Lake Chad
(13 000 km
to 26 000 k

Senegal

Niger

Bén

Orinoco

Salto del Angel

Japurá

Amazon

Marañon

Purus

Madeira

Xingu

Tocantins

São Francisco

Lake Titicaca
(8 340 km²)

Pilcomayo

Paraguay

Paraná

Iguaçu

**SOUTH
AMERICA**

 Great lakes (more than 5,500km²)

Great rivers (more than 1,000km long)

 Extraordinary waterfalls

Major catchment areas

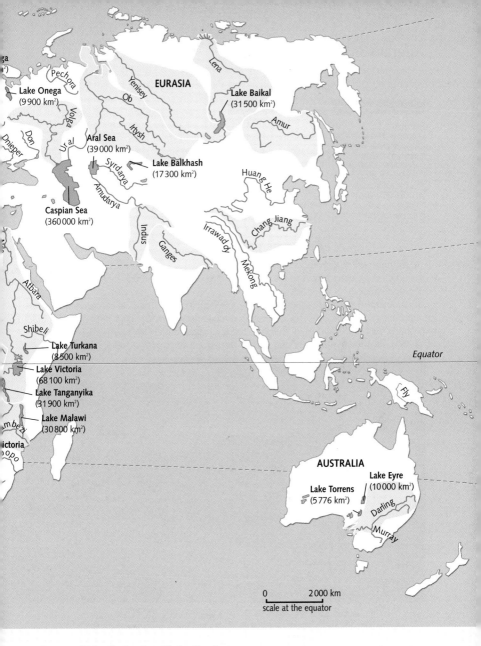

*The area of Lake Chad varies with the flow from
the river feeding into it (the Chari)

Aggravating factors

Many factors can make a flood worse, either by causing a rise in the proportion of run-off water or by facilitating the formation of very dangerous mudflows. Impermeable surfaces (such as roads and car parks) increase run-off, as do some cultivated areas where the ground may be packed hard by the passage of heavy machines. Cultivated land is also liable to erosion. In addition, the destruction of flood plains upstream of inhabited areas removes areas into which the rising waters can spread. Paradoxically, dykes built as flood barriers sometimes create bottlenecks, increasing the rate of the river's flow and making flooding downstream far worse. Poor dam maintenance may also lead to devastation. If a dam breaks the water pours downstream with a violence and speed far greater than would have been the case if the dam had never been built.

Risk prevention

It is impossible to prevent water levels from rising. However, it is possible to try to minimize the amount of water that runs into a river and to prevent secondary factors from making flooding worse.

Preventing the danger requires a good knowledge of the terrain, its composition and morphology, and the constant monitoring of construction work. Dams in particular should be properly built and maintained. Building in flood plains should also be considered with caution. River beds should be dragged, or deepened, since over a period of years deposits of

On 28 January 2002, the village of Thivencelles (France) awoke to find water everywhere. During the night a dyke along a river had burst, flooding around 60 neighbouring houses.

🔍 **On the island of Makeshkali** in Bangladesh, the inhabitants protect themselves against flooding by building seawalls all along the coastline.

alluvium build up, raising the water level. Abandoned river banks can also be dangerous. If the rising river bursts its banks, it may sweep dead tree trunks and other detritus along with it, which can cause blockages or log jams. This generally leads to a very violent flood when the blockage bursts under the pressure of water. To counter problems of this kind, in some countries (such as the USA) artificial flood plains have been created around some rivers. However, afforestation remains essential to increase the capacity of the ground to absorb water and to avoid erosion, particularly in mountainous regions. For similar reasons, farmers are advised to leave harvest residue in the fields, or to plant a cover of winter vegetation. Polluted sites that are liable to flooding must be cleaned to avoid spreading the pollution.

Mudflows

A rising river eventually bursts its banks. The water pours at great speed onto the surrounding land, which may be very liable to erosion. The river sweeps a lot of debris along with it, including stones, gravel, wood and alluvium. This forms a torrent of mud and stones called a mudflow, which is extremely dangerous to people and devastating to buildings and structures.

Waterfalls

Waterfalls are one of nature's most spectacular wonders. But over the long term their incredible power of erosion means they must eventually disappear.

How a waterfall forms

A waterfall occurs at a sudden break in a river bed, where the water suddenly falls vertically. The term 'cascade' is used for small falls, while 'cataract' is used for falls involving very large volumes of water, such as Niagara Falls or Iguaçu Falls.

Waterfalls can be caused by a range of factors. Some are due to a natural mismatch of levels in the river bed, perhaps created by a fault. However, most waterfalls result from rivers flowing over alternately hard and soft rock. In the case of Niagara Falls, for example, the river pours over a natural escarpment formed at the end of the Ice Age around 15,000 years ago. In other cases, such as Victoria Falls on the Zambezi, the step of harder rock may be caused by the presence of hard volcanic lavas within softer, more easily eroded sediments.

The fate of all falls

Waterfalls cause massive erosion. The current carries sand and small stones along with it, which act as an abrasive on the river bed.

The power of erosion depends mainly on the height of the falls, the rate of the river's flow and the type of rock that is being attacked. Erosion is particularly intense at the bottom of the falls, where the water releases an enormous amount of the kinetic energy that gives it its speed. Here it hollows out a large basin, which may be deeper than the falls are high. The water also hollows out the rock behind the falls, undermining the base of the rocky mass above it. If the erosion is powerful enough and the rock is fairly fragile at that point, the step supporting the waterfall will collapse.

This erosion process competes with another, which eats away at the lip of the falls where the water begins its descent. This process results in the waterfall gradually receding upstream. This leads to the formation of a number of basins at the bottom, each corresponding to a period when the falls were stable. Series of this kind can be seen at the

A paradise for aquatic life

Some of the water going over a waterfall is transformed into droplets and vapour which enter the atmosphere. Turbulence considerably increases the amount of gas dissolved within these droplets, which are later returned to the river. In this way the river waters are effectively oxygenated. Fish need oxygen to breathe. Aerobic bacteria, which absorb and break down organic matter and various types of detritus suspended in the water, also need oxygen. Meanwhile, plants and phytoplankton use carbon dioxide to grow by means of photosynthesis. By providing them with abundant quantities of these gases, waterfalls provide a real boost to aquatic life.

Victoria Falls. The Zambezi, which forms a natural border between Zambia and Zimbabwe, hurls 545 million litres of water a minute from a height of 108m, creating a cloud of vapour rising up to 500m into the sky.

Horseshoe Falls at Niagara. Thus, the shape of a waterfall is changing all the time. As the centuries go by, erosion causes the river to flow more gently as the irregularities in the river bed gradually flatten out; eventually the falls disappear completely.

Tides

> Life on the shoreline is governed by the tides. These are generated by gravity and by the pull of the Moon and the Sun on planet Earth.

Influenced by the stars

Every day, the water at the sea shore rises and then retreats. This is the phenomenon we call the tide. High tide is when the sea level reaches its maximum height (covering part of the coastline); low tide is when the sea level is at its minimum height.

At **Mont St Michel** in France, there is an exceptionally big difference between high and low tide (about 14m). But the tide carries a large amount of sediment (700,000m3 per year), which is silting up the bay and bringing the island a little closer to the mainland every day.

The sea level is influenced by the major celestial bodies, obeying the gravitational force they exert. Gravity is a fundamental law of physics, according to which all material bodies attract each other by means of a force proportional to their mass and inversely proportional to the square of the distance between them. In other words, the heavier or closer the bodies are to one another, the stronger the gravity. The Earth is influenced by the Moon, which is light but very close, and the Sun, which is further away but extremely large. The combination of these two influences results in a force that varies according to the respective positions of the Earth, Moon and Sun.

This force affects all parts of the Earth, but its effects are uneven. It is particularly strong at a point on the planet's surface called the 'zenith', then gradually decreases to a minimum point called the 'nadir', which is diametrically opposite the zenith. The main effect of this force is to attract the surface of the water, pulling it out of shape by making the water level rise towards the zenith point.

A cycle of 24 hours and 50 minutes

As the dominant influence is that of the Moon (more than twice as strong as that of the Sun), the zenith moves round as the Earth spins, once a day, or more precisely once every 24 hours and 50 minutes. The Moon completes its orbit around the Earth in 29 days, 12 hours and 44 minutes, so in the 24 hours it takes for the Earth to spin once on its own axis, the Moon moves by an angle of 13° in relation to it. For a zenith high tide to occur at a particular point, the Earth must spin once plus 13°, which it does in 24 hours and 50 minutes.

Centrifugal force

Gravity in itself is not enough to explain the phenomenon of tides. Gravity is a force of attraction exerted between objects such as planets and stars. The reason these do not collide is because another, opposing force is generated by the rotation of bodies in space. This is commonly known as centrifugal force. At the nadir an attraction of the planet's liquid surface can be observed, opposite to that of the zenith. Tides result from the combined action of gravity and centrifugal force.

Tidal disturbance

If the Earth were uniformly covered in water there would be a high tide at the zenith and the nadir. The planet would look like a rugby ball, whose pointed ends would travel round the globe in alignment with the Moon. However, several other factors enter the equation.

▌A risk of bores

In some estuaries the rising tide generates a series of high waves which travel upstream. With an average height of 2.50m, these waves are dangerous to ships and boats. They occur at times of strong tide in estuaries of a particular shape (60 such sites have been identified across the world). The river bed must be gently sloping to allow the wave to form, the estuary must be funnel-shaped to concentrate the effects of the tide and the river must be low – under these conditions the sudden rise in water level cannot be absorbed. In Brazil, bores on the Amazon may travel more than 1,000km upstream. The Mekong has the highest bores (14m).

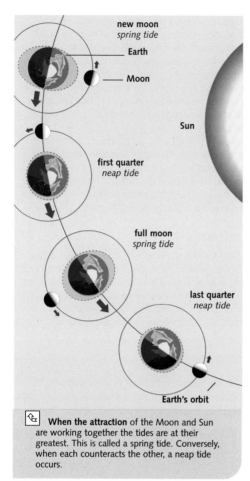

new moon
spring tide

Earth

Moon

Sun

first quarter
neap tide

full moon
spring tide

last quarter
neap tide

Earth's orbit

When the attraction of the Moon and Sun are working together the tides are at their greatest. This is called a spring tide. Conversely, when each counteracts the other, a neap tide occurs.

The Coriolis force due to the spinning of the Earth causes all moving fluids on the planet to veer, and this notably affects the paths of the zenith and nadir. They veer anticlockwise in the northern hemisphere and clockwise in the southern hemisphere, around a point of no tide (called the 'amphidromic' point). Their trajectories are also distorted by the land. Continents block them and friction on the sea bed slows them down, while the shapes of some basins on the sea bed distort them even further.

Variations on a theme

In any given place a tide's size will vary between two extremes. When the tide reaches its maximum height this is called a spring tide and when it is at its minimum level it is a neap tide. This variation is caused by several factors. The force of gravity is inversely proportional to the square of the distance between the Earth and Moon. As the Moon moves in an elliptical orbit round the Earth, the intensity of the tide varies according to the distance of the Moon in the course of the lunar month. When the Moon is at perigee (the point in its orbit when it is closest to the Earth), the force of the tide rises by 20% above the average. Conversely, when it is at apogee (the point in its orbit when it is furthest from the Earth), the force of the tide is reduced by 20%.

While the gravitational pull is inversely proportional to the distance from the attracting body, centrifugal force remains the same at every point on the planet's surface. The combination of these two forces is therefore not symmetrical in relation to the centre of the Earth. Furthermore, the two forces are not exactly parallel, since the Earth's axis is tilted in relation to the plane of the solar system. The sum of the gravitational and centrifugal forces is thus subject to complex variations. This will affect the heighn of any particular tide.

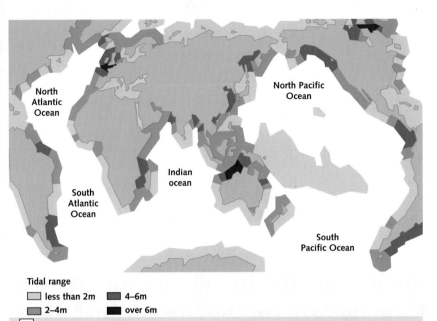

North
Atlantic
Ocean

North Pacific
Ocean

Indian
ocean

South
Atlantic
Ocean

South
Pacific Ocean

Tidal range

☐ less than 2m ■ 4–6m
▨ 2–4m ■ over 6m

The rising movement of the waters caused by the action of gravity and centrifugal force spreads across the ocean in the way that a wave moves across the surface of a lake when you drop a stone into it. The speed of this wave depends on the depth of water. The wave is reflected off the continental shelves, creating disturbances which may reduce or increase its force. The tidal range is the difference in height between the high tide and the low tide before it and is different at every point along the coast. Long bays have greater tidal ranges, while enclosed seas generally have very small tides.

The influence of the Sun

At the same time the Sun also exerts a gravitational pull on the oceans, although this is 2.2 times less than that of the Moon. When the Moon and Sun are aligned with the Earth, their influences act together to create the highest tides of all. These are the equinoctial tides on 21 March and 23 September. Neap tides occur when the Sun and Moon are at right angles to the Earth.

Earth tides

The gravity and centrifugal force that combine to produce the ocean tides also act on the Earth's crust. The distortion they produce is imperceptible to the naked eye because the lithosphere is solid and not very elastic. The range of the Earth tide is zero at the poles, but may reach 40cm in lower latitudes.

The Earth is held in the grip of ice. The presence of ice at the poles acts as a heat regulator, reflecting back solar radiation. The continental glaciers regularize the rates at which rivers flow according to the season, and carve out the rocky landscape as their own weight causes them to move. There have been times when the grip of ice was even tighter: during Earth's ice ages, glaciers and pack ice prevented living creatures from gaining access to a large part of the globe, with important implications for their subsequent evolution.

In the summer, tourists wear swimsuits in Saint Joseph (Michigan). In the winter, the jetty stands over a frozen lake – testimony to the widely varying temperatures of the region.

Ice-bound

Glaciers

Glaciers seem to be fixed in place for all eternity. Yet they are born, they move and they die, carving out the landscape with their force.

Birth of a glacier

Snow is the raw material of a glacier. These flakes of frozen water contain a great deal of air. As the covering of snow thickens in temperatures below freezing, pressure causes the crystal structure to change. The water molecules immobilized in the snowflakes reorganize to fill a smaller volume, forming an extensive geometric network. Recrystallization occurs, resulting in a porous substance somewhere between snow and ice, called névé. Then, under the effect of the snow's weight, the pores close and air no longer circulates. The névé has become ice.

The term 'glacier' refers to any stretch of ice formed from recrystallized snow which lasts from one year to the next and whose own weight causes it to move. In a broader sense it also refers to a range of phenomena – from the layer of ice that covers the Antarctic to a little glacial valley between two mountains in the Alps. Ninety-nine per cent of glaciers are in Antarctica and Greenland. They contain three-quarters of the fresh water on the planet.

When a glacier starts to slip

If the regular sliding of a glacier is impeded by a poor flow of water beneath it, it may be immobilized for several years or even decades. A mass of ice gathers in the accumulation zone and the glacier swells until it reaches a point of imbalance, when it starts to slip down the slope at a rate ten to a hundred times greater than normal. This phenomenon, called a 'surge', affects around 2% of the mountain glaciers in Alaska, central Asia and the Andes around Santiago in Chile.

An eventful life

Glaciers move very slowly, covering a distance of between ten and a few hundred metres a year. This movement is essential for their regeneration: it re-establishes a balance between the accumulation zone, where the glacier grows as a result of falling rain or snow, and the ablation zone, where it shrinks due to evaporation, liquefaction or calving (the disintegration of a cliff of ice).

The glacier is terminated at the extreme end of the ablation zone. In the mountains these zones are rich in rocky debris pushed down by the glacier. By a sea or lake, the end of the glacier – also known as the 'glacier's snout' – is the zone where the layer of ice loses contact with the ground and floats on the water.

Not only is the substance of the glacier constantly renewed, it also goes through periods of expansion followed by periods of retreat. These fluctuations are caused by weather conditions. If more material is added in the accumulation zone than is lost in the ablation zone, the glacier expands. If the reverse is true, it retreats. Today, 10% of the dry land on Earth is covered by glaciers. However, it is estimated that over the last 1.5 million years glaciers have covered an area twice as large as this, then retreated, in a process repeated over twenty times.

Sliding and deformation

Glaciers are constantly becoming distorted and sliding under the effects of their own weight and the influence of the terrain. These

In the 1820s *(left)*, the Mer de Glace glacier in the Alps looked like a thick tongue between the rocky sides of the valley. As recent photographs show *(right)*, its retreat has left indelible marks on the rock.

deformations create crevasses (deep, narrow cracks in the ice) as the glacier moves. Deformation occurs at points of greatest tension in the layer of ice. The upper layers exert a very heavy weight, whereas the lower layers move fairly quickly, carrying the whole glacier with them but generating differential movement within the glacier.

This movement may become accelerated as a result of certain processes. The first is caused by the enormous pressure to which the layer of ice in contact with the ground is subjected. The specific behaviour of water means that it occupies less volume in liquid form than in solid form (as shown by the experiment in which a bottle of water breaks when placed in the freezer). Under high pressure water tends to adopt a structure that takes up less space, in other words it returns to a liquid state. In this way a film of water sometimes forms under the glacier, reducing friction and accelerating movement. The glacier then begins to

GLOSSARY

[Accumulation zone]
Zone in which a glacier gains mass.
[Ablation zone]
Zone in which a glacier loses mass.

Map *(following pages)*

The continental glaciers (also known as ice sheets) covering Greenland and Antarctica, together with the world's valley glaciers, contain almost all the fresh water on the planet. In summer the pack ice, made of frozen seawater, shrinks to a quarter of the area it covers in winter. Its melting allows vital trading to go on in some regions (the Northeast Passage along the Siberian coast and the Northwest Passage along the coast of Alaska).

Pack ice, glaciers and ice sheets

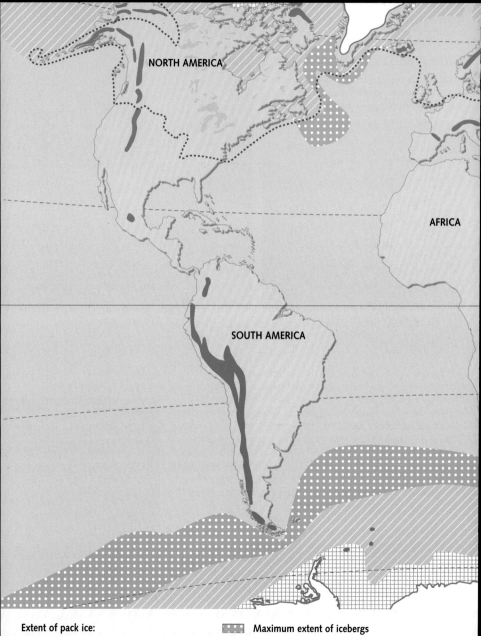

NORTH AMERICA

AFRICA

SOUTH AMERICA

Extent of pack ice:
permanent pack ice
temporary pack ice (in winter)

Maximum extent of icebergs
Ice sheet

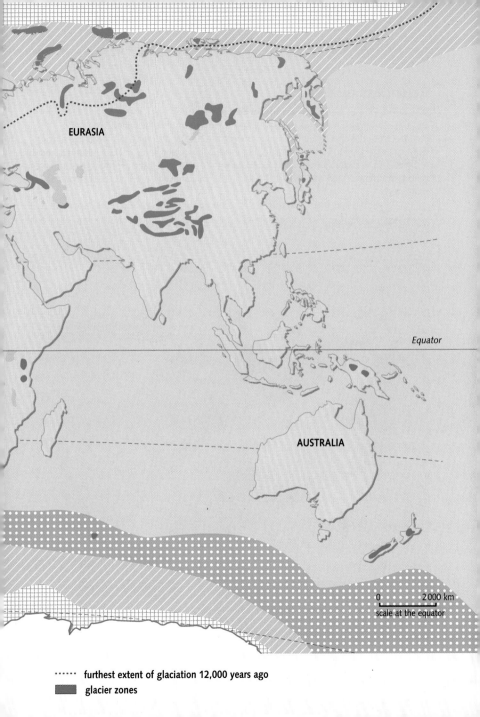

EURASIA

Equator

AUSTRALIA

0   2 000 km
scale at the equator

...... furthest extent of glaciation 12,000 years ago

glacier zones

slide. Acceleration may also occur if there is a sedimentary layer of soft, damp rock under the glacier.

Relentless erosion

As it moves, the glacier shapes the landscape. It carries away rocky material as it goes, causing major glacial erosion and carving out cirques and valleys. Large rocks are incorporated into the glacier as it passes over them or as the rock falls onto the glacier from the valley side. This happens all the more easily when the rock has been cracked and broken. This material is then abandoned when the glacier retreats, forming fields of stones called 'moraines' (pieces of debris the size of a house have sometimes been found in moraines).

This debris that has been more or less incorporated into the mass of the glacier starts to

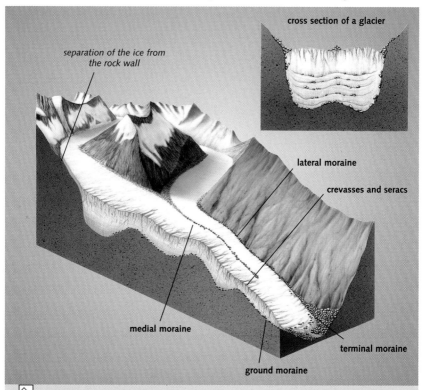

cross section of a glacier

separation of the ice from
the rock wall

lateral moraine

crevasses and seracs

medial moraine

terminal moraine

ground moraine

The glacier tongue pushes forward and erodes the rock, creating lines or fields of rocky debris known as moraines. It advances unevenly, resulting in riegels. The ice itself melts, forming crevasses separated by irregular areas called seracs.

Global warming

Glaciers expand and retreat depending on climatic conditions at the time. In recent years, the current global warming – for which human beings are at least partially responsible – has caused glaciers to retreat considerably. This phenomenon has been measured by scientists in glaciers in the Alps. The glaciers of the Norwegian Svalbard archipelago (consisting largely of the island of Spitzbergen) in the Arctic Circle have also retreated several kilometres. However, the climatic disturbance of global warming has resulted in increased precipitation falling on some glaciers. In western Norway, the glaciers have increased their volume in the last ten years. But the overall effect on glaciers across the globe remains negative.

Glacial erosion is responsible for the unusual shape of the Half Dome, a peak in the Yosemite National Park in California (USA).

act like sandpaper. The abrasion polishes the glacier bed, grinding the rock over which it passes into particles finer than sand. This 'rock flour' can be carried beyond the glacier by melting ice. When it reaches a lake or sea the suspended sediment gives the water a characteristic milky appearance.

GLOSSARY

[Cirque]
Steep-sided, semi-circular depression that has formed above a glacier.
[Moraine]
Area of rocky debris carried and deposited by a glacier.

Pack ice and ice sheets

Ice is a permanent feature of the Earth's high latitudes. Pack ice forms in the sea, ages and renews itself with the passing seasons.

Slow freeze

Pack ice consists of salty water that has frozen at around -2°C (fresh water freezes at 0°C). Freezing takes place in autumn, when the windchill factor varies from -12°C to -15°C. The surface freezes first, but it does so very slowly. As it cools, water becomes denser and tends to sink, while warmer water rises from the depths. This circulation of fluid masses at different temperatures is called 'convection'. It considerably slows the freezing of the pack ice, which can only happen when a column of water is chilled throughout. Freezing therefore occurs first in the shallower zones near the shore. It requires sharp, persistent cold of the kind found in high latitudes. In winter, the polar pack ice covers the centre of the Arctic Ocean and extends as far as the north coast of Iceland.

Several stages

Freezing occurs in three stages. First, ice crystals called frazil appear, making the sea look yellowish due to the modification of the spectrum of colours that it refracts. It becomes more viscous and acquires a greasy consistency. If the cold persists, the frazil gives rise to floating ice pancakes with raised edges that collide on the surface. They measure between 30cm and 3m in diameter and are a few centimetres thick. As they collide the pancakes stick together to form ice floes and then floating pack ice.

The new pack ice differs from the old ice in that it is smooth. The old ice has spent several years floating about (five or six years on average in the

The formation of ice in a salty, mobile medium requires sharp and constant cold. It is in these conditions that the pack ice forms around the Magdalen Islands in Canada.

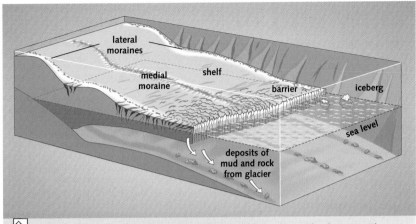

Like all glaciers, ice sheets move slowly, eroding the rock they lie on. They lose material through calving and are regenerated by precipitation.

Arctic Ocean) surviving the summer melt, and has a rolling surface of depressions and elevations. Pack ice is permanent only away from the coast. Near the coasts it melts in summer and vast blocks of ice – icebergs – split off and float away, driven by winds and currents. Most of the pack ice in the Antarctic is like this, and so the ice found in this area is usually first-year ice, or seasonal ice.

Different appearances

Pack ice is established by landfast ice frozen to the beach and built out from frozen tidal pools. This is referred to as the ice foot, and does not move with the tide. It is not attached to the rest of the landfast ice, but is separated by cracks. These are referred to as tidal cracks, and are formed during low tides when the floating part of the ice foot, no longer having support from the water below, bends and fractures. This is a zone of free water where the seals come to breathe. The permanent pack ice is found further away from the shore. This ice is about three metres thick, covers a distance of one or two kilometres a day and lasts for several years. The pack ice is criss-crossed by channels of water called polynyas, which icebreakers seek out on their way through the ice.

Mountains of ice

Unlike pack ice, ice sheets are formed from freshwater precipitation. They are gigantic glaciers that cover continental areas with their icy domes. The two largest ice sheets on the planet cover Greenland and Antarctica. The Greenland ice sheet has an average thickness of 1,500m, rising to a maximum of 3,240m. The average thickness of the Antarctic ice sheet is 2,200m, reaching 4,300m at its highest point. Unlike the glaciers of temperate zones, ice sheets move very slowly.

Snow and hail

Cold, damp weather can give rise to different forms of icy precipitation: snow when the atmosphere is calm, or hail when there is strong movement in the clouds.

Gentle snow

Snowflakes are clusters of ice crystals which form when the atmosphere is cold and damp. When water vapour rises into the atmosphere it quickly condenses into liquid droplets. A cloud forms. If the air temperature is below 0°C, it should cause the water to freeze. However, the force that keeps the water in droplet form, called 'surface tension', prevents it from changing its state. The water is supercooled – in other words, it is liquid water below freezing point. Only the disturbance caused by a collision with very small solid particles (such as dust, sand or smoke) can cause it to change state. If this happens, the water molecules organize themselves into the form of a crystal, which is a regular, repeated accumulation of atoms. In the case of water, the basic crystal is hexagonal (six-sided).

Ice crystals sometimes have surprising shapes which contain points and irregularities.

Variations on a theme

No one snowflake looks like another. When a crystal meets a droplet of supercooled water, this water freezes, adding itself to the crystalline network. This kind of growth naturally fosters irregular shapes since, as a crystal branch grows away from the centre, it encounters a greater degree of humidity in the air around it, enabling it to grow further.

When the snowflake reaches a critical size, it falls. As they fall, snowflakes undergo many transformations. They may melt, be broken up by the wind, collide or combine with other flakes. Their fall is governed by air turbulence, generating an enormous diversity of forms. The longer the fall the larger the snowflake tends to be, as

GLOSSARY

[Crystal]
Solid body characterized by a regular, repeated accumulation of atoms.

These hailstones the size of golf balls fell on Oklahoma in 1978.

long as the air is damp enough to supply it with the material necessary for it to increase in size. Temperature and humidity play a very important part in the shape of snowflakes. Large flakes form when the temperature is close to 0°C and the wind is light. A combination of low temperatures and dry air produces small flakes.

The ups and downs of hailstones

As their structure shows, hailstones form in disturbed air. Most of them have an onion-like structure, with alternating layers of opaque and transparent ice. This alternation of layers is due to the hailstone's many movements back and

Snow and hail also fall in the desert. This photo was taken after a hailstorm in the Kalahari Desert in Namibia.

forth within its cloud. Hailstones form in storm clouds (cumulonimbus) when water solidifies on contact with a speck of dust or an ice crystal. It is then carried towards the top of the cloud, where it grows by incorporating other water molecules. When it becomes too heavy, it falls, but partially melts when it encounters a higher temperature. It may then be carried up to the top again, expanding further. The lower the temperature it encounters, the faster the freezing, preventing air bubbles from escaping, which makes the layer of ice more opaque. When it becomes heavy enough the hailstone – whose size may vary from that of a pea to that of a grapefruit – falls to the ground.

Ice storms

Ice storms occur in very specific conditions. They may leave very serious damage in their wake, as well as a landscape of staggering beauty.

Black ice

Ice storms begin with snow and very strong wind, indicating an encounter between air masses at different temperatures. Then the rain comes. This particular type of rain freezes as soon as it lands on a surface, covering the ground, trees and buildings in a film of black ice, sometimes frost. When the rain persists and the ice builds up, it is called an ice storm. These storms turn roads into skating rinks, break the branches off trees with the weight of ice, bring down electricity cables in the middle of winter and create all kinds of very serious problems.

Ice storms make it impossible to drive a vehicle and also cause serious damage, in particular to electricity and telephone cables.

What causes an ice storm

Ice storms form along a warm front when a mass of warm air penetrates a mass of cold air. The warm air becomes sandwiched between two masses of cold, dry air and this particular configuration gives rise to freezing rain. The warm, humid mass rises into atmospheric regions that are not as dense (drier). It then encounters very low temperatures and freezes, forming snowflakes. These flakes combine and expand until their weight causes them to fall. On the way down they pass back through the warm layer and melt. The water drops continue to fall, passing through the cold layer nearer the ground, but the surface tension that holds them in the form of drops prevents them from freezing. They remain liquid at a temperature below 0°C, a phenomenon called 'supercooling' (laboratory

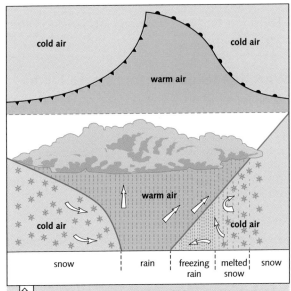

When a mass of warm air is caught between two masses of cold air, the result may be an ice storm, characterized by particular forms of precipitation.

experiments have shown that pure water in the form of very small droplets can remain in this state down to a temperature of –40°C). However, supercooled water is extremely unstable and has only to meet the smallest speck of dust to freeze at once. This is what happens when the water drops meet the ground, or any other cold surface. The crystallization of large drops of supercooled water produces black ice: transparent with no air bubbles, clinging, smooth as glass and extremely slippery.

Cloaked in ice

On 5–9 January 1998, an ice storm of rare intensity travelled across North America. Montreal was cloaked in black ice up to 30cm thick. The resulting damage was considerable. Thirty people died in Canada. Ice destroyed a great many electrical installations, temporarily depriving 60% of the inhabitants of Quebec of electricity. Millions of people were plunged into cold darkness and the supply of drinking water was cut off in certain regions. This area is susceptible to ice storms, as it is here that warm air from the Gulf of Mexico meets ice-cold air from the Arctic.

Ice ages

The recurrence of glacial and interglacial periods on the Earth has had an enormous influence on the evolution of all living things.

When the temperate zones were tundra

Over the last 1.8 million years the Earth has experienced a series of ice ages. During the most pronounced of these periods of intense cold, herds of reindeer grazed on the moss and lichen that grew all over southern Europe. Glaciers stretched as far as Scotland and the northern Netherlands. Ice sheets – some of them 3,000m thick – covered Greenland, North America and Siberia. With so much water held in the ice, sea levels were 100m lower. In the tropics, the forests could not withstand the drought and the deserts expanded. During the subsequent interglacial periods, hippopotamuses wallowed in the River Thames.

Cyclical phenomena

Throughout the Quaternary period (from 1.8 million years ago up to the present), ice ages have succeeded each other at a rate of one every 100,000 years. Each has lasted around 80,000 years, before giving way to a warm period lasting 20,000 years.

We are now reaching the end of an interglacial period. This periodicity is due to variations in the Earth's orbit round the Sun, as shown by the mathematician Milutin Milankovitch in 1924. The Earth follows an elliptical path around the Sun, but this is distorted due to the attraction exerted by neighbouring stars. So the ellipse is more or less elongated and the north-south axis of the planet is more or less tilted in relation to its orbital plane. Also, the Earth does not occupy the same position in relation to the Sun at a

When the ice ages were at their height, North America and most of Europe looked like this Greenland landscape.

At the end of the last ice age, 12,000 years ago, southern Europe was covered in cold steppes and was home to mammoths, woolly rhinoceroses and reindeer. The map above shows how far the ice extended at this time.

'Snowball' Earth

It has been postulated that two phenomenal ice ages have affected the Earth: the first between 760 and 700 million years ago, and the second between 620 and 590 million years ago. In those periods, almost all the sea was covered by ice. Only a few refuge areas near the equator were spared from freezing, enabling a few living creatures – algae and fungi – to survive. The isolation of the animal and plant populations in these ecosystems meant that there was a great diversity of evolving species, and after the ice ages, the planet saw an explosion of life forms. It must have been easy for the survivors to colonize the almost virgin Earth, rapidly adapting to newly diversified habitats.

given time every year. All these parameters influence the amount of solar energy received at different latitudes in different seasons. They modify the circulation of atmospheric and oceanic currents and the whole climate of the planet is disturbed as a result.

Glaciology as proof

In the 1970s, core samples of ice from near the poles and of sediments from marine environments have made it possible to confirm Milankovitch's theory. In the ice cores, bubbles of atmosphere trapped in the ice sheets and shells from marine animals at the bottom of the seas were found to be deposited in successive layers, providing a record of the different climates during different periods.

T he Earth's atmosphere is responsible for the appearance of a great many surprising and fascinating phenomena. These include: mirages, which occur when variations in the density of the atmosphere cause light rays to curve; lightning, flashing across a sky that is dark with electrically charged clouds; and the polar auroras, which we see when a solar wind strikes a layer of the upper atmosphere known as the ionosphere.

The aurora borealis lights up the sky near Fairbanks in Alaska. The rare red colour indicates a phenomenon at very high altitude.

Spectacular skies

Mirages

Mirages are real optical phenomena. They appear when the atmosphere splits into several layers, each with a different density.

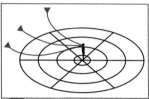

When the ground is overheated, the light rays received by the observer curve towards the ground.

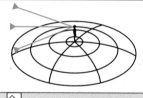

The observer believes that the light rays are straight and has the impression of standing on raised ground.

A story in pictures

All points on the surface of an illuminated object reflect light rays in all directions. When we look at the object, our eye receives some of these rays, which project the image of the object onto the retina, as though it were a miniature cinema screen. The retina membrane consists of a great many sensory receivers which are stimulated by the light and send a signal to the brain, where the information from the light is processed. The image is analysed by specialized areas in the brain, which 'interprets' reality – what we perceive is not strictly reality itself, but the brain's interpretation of it.

Light rays in a hurry

The brain interprets all incidences of light as if they have come in a straight line from the object being looked at. However, this is not always the case. Light travels through different mediums along paths – light rays – which do not necessarily follow a straight line. According to the principles of geometrical optics set out by Pierre de Fermat

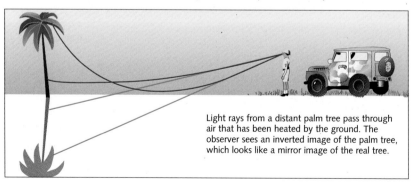

Light rays from a distant palm tree pass through air that has been heated by the ground. The observer sees an inverted image of the palm tree, which looks like a mirror image of the real tree.

Mirages are quite common in the Sahara. Sadly, the oasis is often much farther away than it seems.

in 1650, light takes the path along which it can travel the most quickly. The more dense the medium through which it passes, the more slowly the light will travel. For this reason light rays sometimes take short-cuts that are not straight in order to avoid a medium that is too dense, just as a car driver will get to a meeting more quickly by avoiding roads full of traffic.

Seeing something that is not there

When the ground is at a very different temperature from the atmosphere – above sunlit pack ice or above the desert sand, for example – the air will form into non-homogeneous layers with gradually rising or falling temperatures. The density of a gas is directly linked to its temperature: the hotter it is the greater volume it fills and the lower its density. In the desert, the density of the atmosphere varies enormously between the layers in direct contact with the ground (very hot) and the layers at eye-level (cooler). When the ground is overheated, light rays on their way to the retina will therefore pass through the less dense layers nearer the ground, and will be refracted. The brain then interprets the image as though the light had travelled in a straight line from the source, making it appear lower than it really is. It sometimes happens that several light rays reach the eye, each representing a different pathway the light can take to reach the eye. In such cases several mirages appear, none of which corresponds to reality.

Map *(following pages)*

Polar auroras are very rare in the middle latitudes, but are common near the poles, as the Earth's geomagnetic shield is much weaker there. Due to the strong vertical movements of the air inside clouds above the continents, thunder and lightning are more frequent there than over the oceans. The intertropical convergence zone is also home to intense electrical storms.

Gravitational mirages

In his theory of general relativity, Einstein assumed that massive objects (such as stars) would cause space-time to curve. The path of any particle, and particularly the photons that make up light rays, would be modified on approaching such objects, giving rise to 'gravitational mirages'. Proof of this was provided in 1979, with the first observation of the double image of a distant galaxy. The study of gravitational lens effects now makes it possible to map the universe by revealing the presence of massive invisible objects.

Polar auroras and lightning

NORTH AMERICA

SOUTH AMERICA

Density of lightning (number of flashes/km²/year)

0.12–0.30	1.20–3
0.30–1.20	3–6

6–15	over 30
15–30	

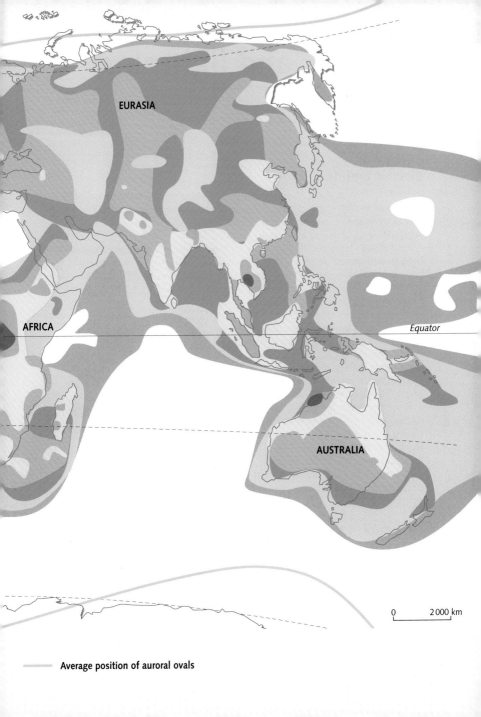

EURASIA

AFRICA

Equator

AUSTRALIA

0   2 000 km

Average position of auroral ovals

Thunder and lightning

Lightning is both beautiful and dangerous. It shoots wildly through the sky and hits the ground at a point that is impossible to predict, provoking fear and wonder as it strikes.

Electric clouds

Lightning is created deep inside storm clouds. These huge dark cumulonimbus clouds float along at an altitude of around 2km and may rise more than 10km into the air. Within their anvil-shaped mass they hold hundreds of thousands of tonnes of water in the form of supercooled droplets and ice crystals.

Storm clouds are particularly unstable, as they are subject to great differences in temperature caused by the meeting of two atmospheric masses or by the heat that has been stored in the ground (these latter cases are known as heat bursts). This instability translates into a convection movement that can reach speeds of 70kph. The friction between the water drops and the ice particles creates electricity.

When the difference of potential created in this way is too great, an electrical discharge results. Ninety per cent of these discharges occur inside the cloud; the rest reach the ground. A 'pre-discharge', which is not very bright, leaps downwards. When this 'tracer' is about 10m from the ground, a rising discharge comes up to meet it. Their meeting creates a very bright electrical arc which plunges to the ground down the channel that has been created. Sometimes, particularly in the mountains, the first discharge rises, in which case the lightning descends.

Effects of lightning

On average, there are 100 bolts of lightning every second worldwide. Every year in France around a million impacts are recorded; these cause about 30 deaths and 15,000 fires.

The damage is due to the large amount of energy that lightning contains. The electrical discharge of a lightning bolt is around one

A lightning bolt caused part of this church roof in a French village to explode.

Lightning follows a random path across the sky, making it impossible to predict. Above, lightning over San Francisco.

million volts, with a lighting power equivalent to that of a hundred million ordinary light bulbs. The energy carried in the bolt turns into light (lightning itself), sound energy (thunder) and heat. The electrical arc reaches a temperature of around 30,000°C.

Material damage is caused mainly by the heating of structural parts of buildings and by electromagnetic radiation, which damages electronic equipment and computers. Effects on human beings vary greatly. People who are struck by lightning may be unhurt, while their clothes are vaporized. This happens when the discharge is strong enough to move along the skin without passing through the body. If the discharge of electricity and heat does pass through any organs, these can be seriously damaged.

Protection

The classic lightning conductor has proved its worth in protecting buildings. Basically a metal rod connected to the ground, it channels the lightning down into the earth. For the last twenty years or so, scientists have been trying to induce lightning using a laser beam which, by ionizing the atmosphere, would create a preferential path for the electrical discharge. Progress with these beams should lead to success in the next few years.

Ball lightning

Balls of lightning are rare. They are about 30cm across, of medium brightness, and spin at about 1m above the ground for a few dozen seconds before fading or bursting. Although their existence is well documented, they remain a mystery to scientists.

Polar auroras

The aurora borealis and aurora australis can be seen near the North Pole and South Pole respectively. They are the visible traces of collisions between the solar wind and our atmosphere.

Shimmering curtains of light

The polar auroras look like shimmering curtains hanging in the sky in the high latitudes around the polar regions. They are extremely rare in the medium latitudes. They are called aurora borealis in the north and aurora australis in the south. These veils of light seem to start at an altitude of about 100km and come down to a height of a few hundred metres, where the density of the atmosphere puts an end to the phenomenon. They are generally less than 1km thick, but they can encircle the globe, covering thousands of kilometres. They can quickly change shape, intensity and location. Although it is hard for our eyes to perceive colours at night, they generally look white, tinged with green, yellow, blue, or – very rarely – red. They usually last for a few minutes, but can sometimes last for a few hours.

The solar particles come into contact with the ionosphere, the outer layer of the atmosphere, near the poles

In the solar wind

The polar auroras are the visible evidence of the impact of the solar wind on the Earth's atmosphere. The upper atmosphere of the Sun consists of particles (electrons and protons) heated to several million degrees. At such temperatures the particles move very fast, around 150kps for protons and 5,000kps for the lighter electrons. When they move like this, the electrons tend to escape the Sun's gravity and disperse in space, taking a plasma of protons and a few electrically charged atoms (notably helium) with them. This plasma is continually escaping from the Sun, forming the wind in which the whole solar system is bathed. Its speed and density depend on its source; they are greater when the particles come from active regions in the Sun, such as sunspots or protuberances. When it reaches the Earth's orbit, after about four days of travelling through space, the solar wind contains about five particles per cubic centimetre.

Bound for the poles

The Earth is surrounded by a magnetic field generated by the movements of its liquid outer core. When the electrically charged solar particles approach the Earth, they are caught in the Earth's magnetic field, which draws them towards the magnetic poles. There, they come into contact with the atoms of the ionosphere, which is the outer layer of the Earth's atmosphere. These collisions stimulate the atoms (mainly oxygen and nitrogen), causing them to redistribute the energy they have stored up. The wavelength of the resulting radiation depends on the molecule and its chemical state. The oxygen atoms, at an altitude of 100km, reflect a yellow-green light and, if the collision happens further up, a red light. At low altitudes the nitrogen atoms give out a pale red light. At higher altitudes, the light turns to violet. In effect, the polar auroras reflect the composition of the upper atmosphere.

The light of the polar auroras is generally yellow and green – characteristic of the energy released when electrically charged particles collide with oxygen atoms present at an altitude of 100km.

The polar auroras are not unique to Earth, as this picture of Jupiter shows.

Whether silvery gleams in the night sky or sudden showers of stones, comets and meteorites have long been interpreted as portents of disaster. Today, however, the study of these phenomena has become an important matter for 21st-century scientists. Perhaps they will provide us with answers to the questions: why did some species become extinct and, more importantly, why is there life on our planet? When the Earth came into being, comets and asteroids interacted with the planet in a remarkable way.

The spectacular Leonid meteorite showers in November 1999 and November 2003 were due to the passage of the Swift–Tuttle Comet shortly before.

Cosmic phenomena

Comets, messengers from the skies

Comets are still seen as bringers of messages. Once used to predict the future, today they are studied in the hope that they will illuminate the past.

Comets through the ages

What are comets and what are they made of? This is the question that the Ancient Greeks – who gave them the name kometes, meaning 'long-haired star' – were asking 1,500 years ago. A satisfactory answer was not provided until the late 20th century.

In the 6th century BC, the Pythagoreans regarded comets as heavenly objects which moved in similar ways to the planets, and whose return could therefore be predicted. In this they were correct. However, two centuries later Aristotle saw things very differently. He believed that comets were meteors which ignited in the upper atmosphere, similar to fires or earthly vapours. Since they belonged to the sublunary world, they were not real objects, but merely fiery apparitions or illusions.

It was this theory that prevailed for more than

The Bayeux Tapestry. In 1066, King Harold of England saw a comet appear in the sky and took it as an omen that he would lose the battle of Hastings against the Duke of Normandy, William the Conqueror.

Good or bad omen?

The Babylonians believed that a comet that disappeared southwards presaged a good harvest. The auspicious births of Caesar and Mithidrates were supposed to have been announced by the passage of a comet brighter than the Sun. Conversely, tradition has it that the deaths of the Roman emperor Vespasian and the prophet Mohammed were caused by the passing of a comet. The list of comet-related omens, both good and bad, is endless. Such beliefs continued into the early 20th century, when many saw the arrival of Halley's Comet in 1910 as heralding World War I.

With its two clearly visible tails – one blue (consisting of ionized gas) and the other yellow (containing dust) – the Hale–Bopp Comet appeared in the winter sky in 1997.

2,000 years, until the end of the 16th century. In the year 1597, after spending 12 years studying them, the Danish astronomer Tycho Brahe announced that comets went far beyond the Moon and were material bodies like planets. The study of comets could at last proceed on a firm scientific basis.

The return of the comets

Observing a comet in 1680, Sir Isaac Newton noted that it followed the Sun both in the evening and in the morning; he thought it was attracted by the Sun and moved round it. He calculated its path and showed that comets travelled round the Sun in orbits that were either elliptical (in other words in a more or less elongated flat curve, with the Sun as one focus) or hyperbolic (with a second focus located in infinity, in which case the comet never returns).

In 1705, Edmund Halley noted striking similarities between observations of comets made in 1682, 1606 and even 1531. He established that they all referred to the same comet, which returned every 76 years, and calculated that it would next return in the year 1758. This was the first time that a comet's return was successfully predicted. It was given the name Halley's Comet.

Map *(following pages)*

The remains of comets and asteroids that are not completely burnt up in the atmosphere fall to Earth. Sometimes the impact leaves a deep crater, called an astrobleme, whose scar is still visible millions of years later. In statistical terms, 70% of such objects fall into the oceans, and do not therefore feature on the map.

 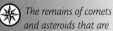

Meteorite craters

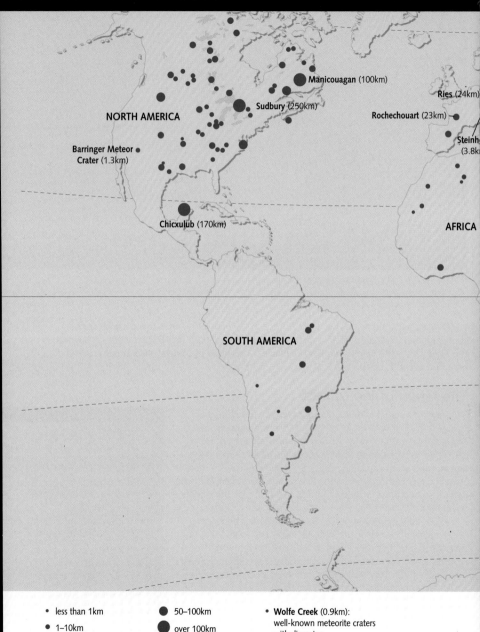

NORTH AMERICA

Manicouagan (100km)

Ries (24km)

Sudbury (250km)

Rochechouart (23km)

**Steinh
(3.8k

**Barringer Meteor
Crater** (1.3km)

Chicxulub (170km)

AFRICA

SOUTH AMERICA

- less than 1km
- 1–10km
- 10–50km
- 50–100km
- over 100km
- **Wolfe Creek** (0.9km):
  well-known meteorite craters
  with diameter

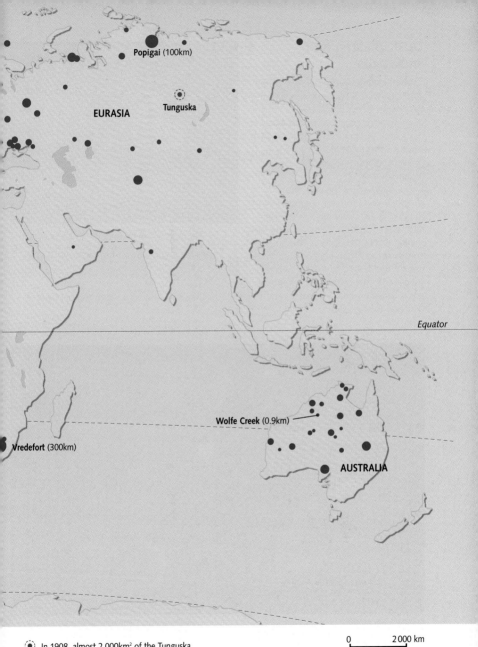

Popigai (100km)

EURASIA

Tunguska

Wolfe Creek (0.9km)

Vredefort (300km)

AUSTRALIA

Equator

In 1908, almost 2,000km² of the Tunguska region was devastated when a fragment from a meteorite or comet exploded just above the ground.

0   2 000 km
scale at the equator

Dust, plasma and snowballs

When a comet is on the edge of the solar system it is an enormous ball of dirty snow, a few kilometres in diameter. Composed of frozen water, it has a kind of dark, dusty crust made of various substances including carbon, oxygen, sulphur, silicon and magnesium.

As it approaches the Sun, this snowball starts to melt, leaving behind it a double tail. One tail is yellowish and formed by dust flying off with the melted water, the other is bluish and consists of gas that escapes from the comet and is ionized by the sunlight (hence the blue colour). This ionized

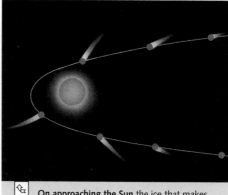

On approaching the Sun the ice that makes up much of a comet starts to melt, leaving behind a double tail of debris which may spread over millions of kilometres.

gas is called plasma. The solar wind always causes the two tails to point in the opposite direction to the Sun.

Comets from the Oort cloud have very elongated orbits outside the orbital plane of the planets.

Oort cloud ...

After the planetary system was formed, a large number of rocky objects which were orbiting beyond the paths of the four giant planets were expelled to the edge of the solar system by their gravitational influence. The result was a kind of halo of various objects around the entire solar system, orbiting at a distance of between 0.1 and 0.5 light-years. This is the Oort cloud.

Sometimes it happens that another star passing near the Sun, or the nearby presence of a nebula of gas and dust, disturbs the Oort cloud and expels some elements – comets – in the direction of the Sun. These comets have very elongated elliptical orbits, indeed sometimes they are hyperbolas (in which case they never return). At first these 'young' comets take a very long time to return (for example the Hale–Bopp Comet, seen in 1997, will not return until 6300). However, over time they 'age', slowed down by the gravity around the Sun each time they return. Gradually their orbit shrinks and they return more frequently. Halley's Comet, which returns every 76 years, is comparatively old, although not as old as Encke's Comet, which comes back every 3.3 years.

This photo of Halley's Comet taken by the Giotto probe in 1986 shows the dirty snowball that forms the comet's head.

Comets and the Earth

When the Earth was still new and had no atmosphere, it was bombarded by millions of comets. The impact traces have now been erased by earthquakes and volcanoes. It is thought that ice brought by the comets contributed to the filling of the oceans. The Earth is still showered with thousands of former comets but, as they are now broken into small pieces, the atmosphere burns them up almost completely, transforming the fragments into 'shooting stars' and allowing only tiny pieces of dust known as meteorites to reach the ground.

... or Kuiper belt?

In the 1990s it was discovered that objects were escaping from another 'space store' situated beyond Neptune, known as the Kuiper belt. These objects also become comets (Kuiper comets) whose orbital plane merges with that of the planets. Because they were formed at the same time as the solar system, Oort and Kuiper comets could provide us with a great deal of information about the conditions that existed when the various planets were created, including the Earth.

Meteorites from comets

Whether we experience it as a rock hitting the Earth or as a bright streak in the sky (a 'shooting star'), almost every meteorite derives from a comet.

After the comet, the shower

In its orbit round the Sun, the Earth encounters dust, stones and sometimes rocks which are passing through our solar system. Some of these objects come from asteroids, but most come from comets.

As it nears the Sun, a comet starts to burn up, losing an enormous amount of material (20–30 tonnes per second). This is mainly water and dust, but also includes fragments of rock. After the comet has passed, this debris remains in orbit around the Sun for a while, before dispersing. When the Earth's orbit crosses such a concentration of comet fragments, the Earth is subjected to a 'shower' of debris. Today, we can link almost any meteorite swarm to the passage or path of a comet – for example, the Perseids and the Swift–Tuttle Comet in July and August or the Leonids and the Temple Comet in November.

An average of 250 tonnes of comet debris fall to Earth every day. On contact with the atmosphere these fragments (or meteorites) burst into flames, leaving an incandescent trail.

Two hundred and fifty tonnes every day

Crossing the debris left by a comet at a distance of only 150 million kilometres from the Sun, the Earth is sprinkled with showers of meteorites, of which around 400,000 tonnes of fragments reach the ground every year (about 250 tonnes per day). These figures seem very large – but so is the Earth. From a statistical point of view, this means that, on average, only one meteorite weighing more than 500g falls on each square kilometre in a million years. However, we know of around ten accidents involving meteorites that have either killed people or destroyed roofs in the last three hundred years.

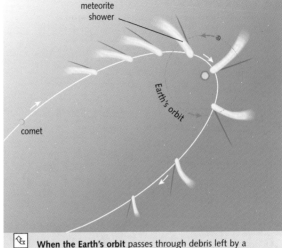

meteorite shower

Earth's orbit

comet

When the Earth's orbit passes through debris left by a comet, this causes a meteorite shower.

Shooting stars …

When a piece of comet debris penetrates the Earth's atmosphere, it is travelling at 50,000–250,000kph. It has become a meteorite. On contact with the upper strata of the atmosphere, at an altitude of around 80km, the meteorite is subject to very violent friction with the mesosphere (one of the outer atmospheric layers), which slows it down considerably and makes it burn very brightly. The air is electrified by the passage of the burning meteorite, which leaves a blue trail behind it. It is this that we call a 'shooting star' or, more scientifically, a meteoroid. Shooting stars are not real stars at all, but simply stones melting in our atmosphere.

Usually, the friction between meteorite and atmosphere is enough to burn the meteorite up completely. However, it can happen that some part of it falls all the way down to Earth.

GLOSSARY

[Meteor]
Any phenomenon (except clouds) observed in the atmosphere, particularly the luminous trail of a meteorite entering the atmosphere.

… or holes in the ground

When it hits the ground, the meteorite makes a crater, whose appearance depends on the object's mass and how fast it was travelling. This crater is called an astrobleme. If the object is fairly large, and therefore moving very fast, all or some of its kinetic energy is converted into heat on impact and the meteorite disintegrates completely, leaving what is called an 'explosion' crater.

Meteor Crater in Arizona (USA) has a diameter of 1.3km. It was formed by the impact of a ferrous meteorite 25m in diameter, which hit the Earth 30,000 years ago at a speed of 15kps.

GLOSSARY

[Astrobleme]
Crater formed when an object moving through space collides with a planet. The term comes from the Greek astron, 'star', and blema, 'wound'.

If, on the other hand, its mass is only a few kilos or tens of kilos, it is not travelling so fast when it hits the ground. In these cases, the meteorite creates an impact crater around it and remains more or less intact. Currently we know of around a hundred large astroblemes created by meteorites, including the famous Meteor Crater in Arizona, which is 1,300m across and 200m deep. This crater was created 30,000 years ago by a meteorite about 25m in diameter.

Every shower has its radiant

Meteorites give rise to shooting stars all year round, but there are some periods when they appear in greater numbers – when the Earth passes through meteorite swarms left by the passage of various comets.

Each meteorite swarm is named after a particular constellation, such as the Bootids after the constellation Boötes, or the Perseids after Perseus. In the night sky, every meteor from the same swarm appears to be coming from the same point. This point is called the swarm's 'radiant'. When this convergent point appears in or near a

Can they kill?

There is only one recorded instance of a person being killed by a meteorite. This was a Franciscan monk in 1644. However, large astroblemes suggest that meteorite showers can sometimes be very violent. The extinction of the dinosaurs around 65 million years ago is thought to be linked to a hail of comet debris. The animals would not have been killed by the meteorites themselves, but by the millions of tonnes of earth that the impact sent into the atmosphere, causing 75% of the species on the planet to die out.

constellation, the meteorite swarm takes that constellation's name. So in order to see the greatest number of shooting stars during the period of a particular meteorite shower, we should look towards the constellation concerned.

Finding meteorites

Unless the impact crater is large, it is very hard to find meteorites on the ground. These little stones – some containing iron, others not – are almost impossible to identify among all the other stones around them. This is why professional meteorite hunters, seeking to study the chemical make-up of these witnesses to the birth of the solar system, go to the Arctic or to Antarctica, where meteorites are easy to spot on the stretches of white ice. Similarly, many amateurs find them on mountain glaciers in summer.

Though a million years old, the Wolfe Creek crater in Australia remains perfectly preserved. It was caused by a meteorite weighing several thousand tonnes.

Main meteorite swarms in 2003

Meteor shower	Active Period	Max Hourly Rate	Parent Body
Quadrantids	1-5 Jan	120	unknown
Lyrids	16-25 Apr	18	Thatcher
Eta-Aquarids	19 Apr-28 May	60	Halley
Southern Delta-Aquarids	12 Jul-19 Aug	20	unknown
Perseids	17 Jul- 24 Aug	110	Swift-Tuttle
Orionids	2 Oct – 7 Nov	20	Halley
Leonids	14 – 21 Nov	100+	Temple
Puppid-Velids	1-15 Dec	10	unknown
Geminids	7-17 Dec	120	Phaethon

Asteroids

Residue from the formation of the planets, asteroids travel beyond the orbit of Mars. But sometimes one of them passes alarmingly close to the Earth. These are called Earth-crossing asteroids.

Some 4.6 billion years ago

When the Sun was reaching its fully formed state, some of the material that had not been incorporated into it went into an orbit shaped like a flat disc. Very quickly the dust elements combined to form bodies quite similar to the asteroids of today. There were a great number of these and they collided with each other, combining to form the planets. Residual material was expelled towards the outside of the solar system, forming the Kuiper belt and Oort cloud. Other fragments, the asteroids, remained trapped within the solar system.

Between Mars and Jupiter: the asteroid belt

The distances between the planets of the solar system follow a geometrical progression. According to the Titius-Bode law, there should be a planet between Mars and Jupiter, around 400 million kilometres from the Sun. Instead, at a distance of 300–600 million kilometres, there is a vast asteroid belt. It is assumed that this was a planet that never formed, the nearby huge mass of Jupiter preventing any other large body from forming in the vicinity. Because these asteroids are too small to see with the naked eye, with average diameters of only a few kilometres and ill-defined shapes, they long remained unknown to us. They were brought to the attention and concern of the wider public only when it was discovered that some pass very close to the Earth.

The threat of Earth-crossing asteroids

In the cartoon adventure *Explorers on the Moon*, Tintin and his friends encounter the asteroid Adonis far from the asteroid belt. This is an Earth-crossing asteroid – that is, an asteroid whose orbit crosses that of the Earth, sometimes even passing between the Earth and the Moon. Earth-crossing asteroids are thought to come from the furthest regions of the asteroid belt, having been expelled in the direction of the Sun by Jupiter. Once launched into space, they are subject to the influence of various planets and may follow very eccentric paths. More than a hundred such asteroids have been identified today, with sizes close to or larger than 1m, the largest so far identified being Geographos

The **Earth-crossing** asteroid Eros, photographed in 2000, is 34km long and 13km wide.

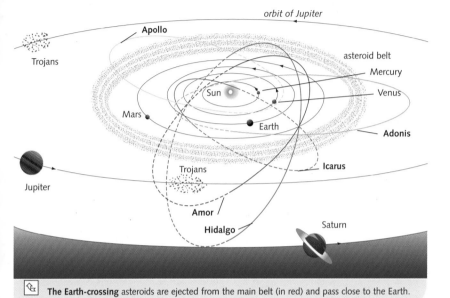

The Earth-crossing asteroids are ejected from the main belt (in red) and pass close to the Earth.

(5.1 by 1.8km). If one of these were to hit the Earth – as, statistically speaking, will happen once every 60 million years – there would be a major cataclysm, with the creation of a crater 10–200km wide.

Impact of an Earth-crossing asteroid

The impact of an asteroid more than 500m in diameter would have devastating effects on the Earth's inhabitants. According to astronomers' calculations, there are no serious threats for the next 50 years, although on 7 August 2027 the asteroid 1999 AN10 is due to pass the Earth at a distance of 'only' 400,000km. However, we can console ourselves with the thought that, as the oceans cover 70% of the Earth's surface, that is where 70% of asteroids end up.

Many kinds of asteroids

There are 18 kinds of asteroids, classified according to their distance from the Sun. Generally speaking, the materials they are made of are less dense the further away from the Sun they are. The asteroids closest to the Sun are often ferrous or rocky (containing mainly silicate minerals). Further away, at a distance of 400–600 million kilometres, they are made of carbon, organic compounds and a few silicates. Further still, near Jupiter, most are formed of organic compounds and sometimes various kinds of ice.

As the Earth orbits the Sun and the Moon orbits the Earth, it sometimes happens that the three line up, creating an eclipse of either Sun or Moon. Nothing could be more natural than the phenomenon of the eclipse, in which one body passes in front of another, partially or completely obscuring it. Nothing could be more spectacular either – or more terrifying in the days when people did not yet know why the daylight should suddenly turn to darkness, or the Moon gradually turn red. In the 5,000 years since the development of writing, thousands of accounts of such events have been set down.

Total eclipse of the Sun, photographed in India on 24 October 1995.

Eclipses

The causes of eclipses

Eclipses seem to be a very straightforward phenomenon. However, very specific conditions of size, distance and alignment are required in order for them to occur.

The right size and distance

Because the Earth follows an elliptical path around the Sun, the distance between the two varies between 147 million and 152 million kilometres. The Sun has a diameter of 1.4 million kilometres, so its apparent diameter as seen from the Earth fluctuates between an angle of 31min 28s and an angle of 32min 31s. This difference in angular measurement results from the distance between the Earth and the Moon varying between 356,000km and 406,000km. With a linear diameter of 3,500km, the Moon seen from the Earth has an angular diameter between 29min 22s and 34min 8s. This similarity in the two apparent diameters means that every time the Moon passes between the Earth and the Sun at a point when its diameter appears larger than that of the Sun, the Moon eclipses the Sun. During the eclipse of 1999, for example, the angular diameter of the Sun was 31min 34s and that of the Moon 32min 28s. Where eclipses of the Moon are concerned, the phenomenon is simpler. When the Moon is on the other side of the Earth from the Sun, the umbra of the Earth, which is 9,000km wide when it falls on the Moon, covers all of it. But then we have to ask, why do we not see an eclipse of the Sun and Moon every lunar month?

Perfect alignment

For one object to eclipse another, our eyes and the two objects must all be lined up along the same sight line, in other words on the same

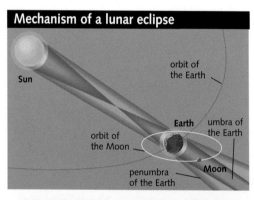

Mechanism of a lunar eclipse

Sun

orbit of the Earth

orbit of the Moon

Earth

umbra of the Earth

penumbra of the Earth

Moon

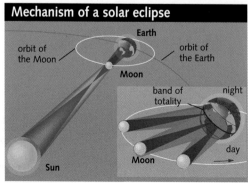

Mechanism of a solar eclipse

Earth

orbit of the Moon

orbit of the Earth

Moon

band of totality

night

day

Moon

Sun

Several types of eclipse

The term 'eclipse' covers a wide range of phenomena. During lunar eclipses the Moon does not completely disappear, but remains lit to varying degrees and with different colours. During solar eclipses the Sun disappears completely in some places on Earth and partially in others (when the Moon hides only part of the Sun). If the Moon is too far from the Earth during a solar eclipse, it does not completely obscure the Sun, but leaves a ring of light. This is called an annular or 'ring' eclipse.

When the Moon is too far from the Earth there is an annular eclipse of the Sun (above, in Morocco in April 1994).

plane. However, the Moon does not orbit the Earth in exactly the same plane as that in which the Earth orbits the Sun (which is called the 'ecliptic plane'). The Moon's plane forms an angle of 5.9° with the ecliptic plane. Eclipses are possible because the plane of the lunar orbit is slowly pivoting, on an axis that is perpendicular to the Earth's orbital plane, in a cycle lasting 18.61 years. Thus, it can happen during this period that the Earth, Moon and Sun are aligned on several different occasions, on what is called 'the line of nodes'. If, on one of these occasions, the Moon is at the right distance from the Earth, then and only then can we see a total eclipse of the Sun.

Map (following pages)

Once the movements of the Moon around the Earth and of the Earth around the Sun are known, it is possible to predict the date and duration of solar eclipses as well as the width of their band of totality (the band defining those places where a total eclipse is visible). However, this requires complex calculations that were not mastered until the 18th century. Eclipses of the Moon are easier to predict.

Saros

GLOSSARY

[Line of nodes]
Line joining the points of intersection between the orbital planes of the Sun and the Moon or the Earth. In the case of eclipses, this is the line of intersections of the Moon's orbital plane with the ecliptic plane.

In practice, the lunar orbit shows irregularities which mean that the cycle of 18.61 years is reduced to 18 years, 11 days and 8 hours. This is called the 'saros' cycle. For every saros there is a corresponding eclipse of the Sun at a particular latitude – but not at the same point. A saros is not a round number of days, due to the extra 8 hours. After 18 years and 11 days, an eclipse occurs 8 hours later than the previous eclipse, in other words at 120° further west.

Eclipses of the Sun

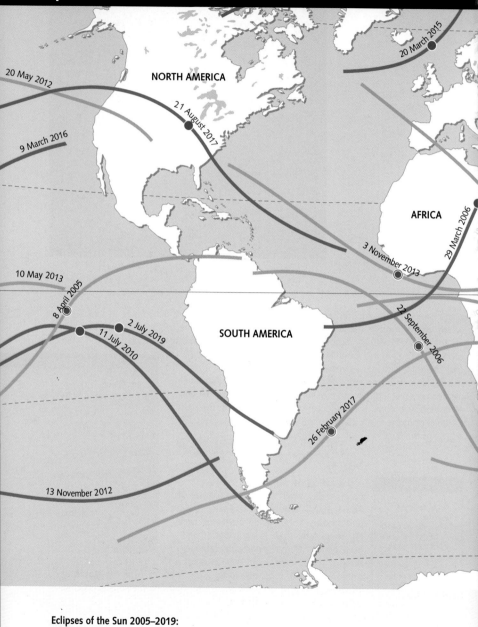

NORTH AMERICA

20 May 2012

9 March 2016

21 August 2017

20 March 2015

AFRICA

29 March 2006

3 November 2013

10 May 2013

8 April 2005

22 September 2006

2 July 2019

11 July 2010

SOUTH AMERICA

26 February 2017

13 November 2012

Eclipses of the Sun 2005–2019:
path of central point of the total eclipse
path of central point of the annular eclipse

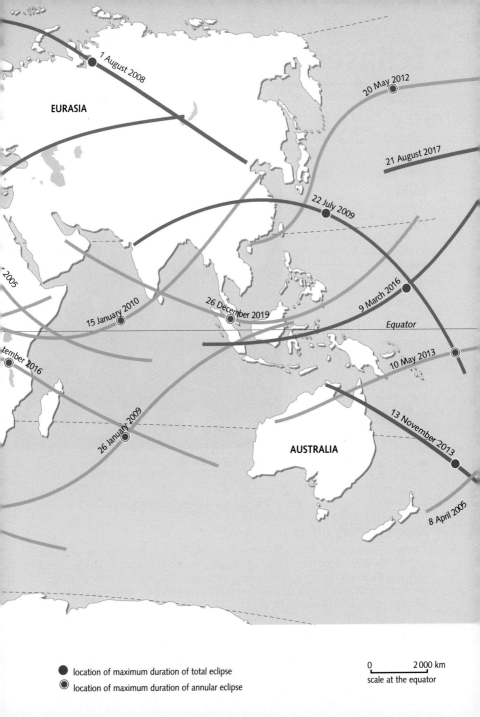

EURASIA

1 August 2008

20 May 2012

21 August 2017

22 July 2009

9 March 2016

26 December 2019

Equator

15 January 2010

10 May 2013

tember 2016

26 January 2009

13 November 2013

AUSTRALIA

8 April 2005

2005

● location of maximum duration of total eclipse

◉ location of maximum duration of annular eclipse

0   2 000 km

scale at the equator

Eclipses of the Sun

The disappearance of the Sun in the middle of the day is one of the most dramatic events human beings can witness. It is accompanied by many extraordinary phenomena.

The arrival of the Moon

A solar eclipse begins when the Moon starts slowly encroaching on the Sun's face from the right. To follow its progress one must wear special glasses to avoid permanent damage to the eyes. It is extremely dangerous to look directly at the Sun, and sunglasses offer no protection at all. There is not an appreciable drop in sunlight intensity until the eclipse is close to totality, when the Moon covers 90% of the Sun's surface. As the Moon passes in front of the Sun, a strange phenomenon can sometimes be seen on the ground. Spots of light in the shade of trees take on an elongated, elliptical shape,

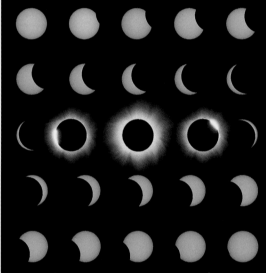

Course of the total solar eclipse of 11 August 1999 in France. The pictures were taken at intervals of about 5 minutes.

and have a section missing on one side, like the partially eclipsed Sun.

Diamond ring effect

A few seconds or tens of seconds before the totality phase, a few luminous spots appear on the edge of the Sun. These spots, called 'Baily's beads', are caused by the passage of the last rays of sunlight across the relief of the lunar surface. The last spot is the brightest, because darkness has already covered the sky. This phenomenon, which lasts only 3–5 seconds, is called the 'diamond ring effect'.

Total eclipse of the Sun photographed in Chile on 3 November 1994. The Sun does not look dark but seems to be shining. This is because the halo of the solar corona has overexposed the film at that point.

During the totality phase

At last the Moon covers the entire surface of the Sun. This is the totality phase, during which protective glasses should not be removed. It is dark, or almost dark; the brightest stars can be seen in the sky, as can shooting stars in some cases. There are a great many phenomena to observe during the brief totality phase, which lasts only 7 minutes and 6 seconds at its longest, and is often much shorter, barely 2 or 3 minutes.

Once the solar disc has been covered, a large, irregular halo of silvery light appears. This is the solar corona – the Sun's atmosphere – which extends for several million kilometres. Closer to the disc we can also see a thin, pink-tinged ring; this is the chromosphere, from which long jets of burning gas, the solar protuberances, sometimes shoot out.

Throughout the phase when the Sun is obscured by the Moon, the temperature on Earth drops very quickly, by several degrees in a few seconds, and a fresh wind rises. A strange silence falls over the natural world: birds stop singing and many animals try to lie down and go to sleep.

Two hundred and twenty-eight solar eclipses

A total eclipse of the Sun requires the Earth, Moon and Sun to be perfectly aligned and the apparent diameter of the Moon to be at least equal to or more than that of the Sun, so that it completely covers it. There were 228 partial or total eclipses of the Sun in the 20th century.

Eclipses of the Moon

Although they happen gradually and do not suddenly turn day into night or night into day, lunar eclipses are still a spectacular sight.

Umbras and penumbras

The Sun is the only body in our solar system which emits its own light. All the other bodies, including the Earth and the Moon, reflect the Sun's rays. A lunar eclipse is viewed in a very different way to a solar eclipse. Like all objects lit on one side by the sun, the Earth has an area of half-shadow or 'penumbra' behind it (on the 'night' side), with a darker inner region called the 'umbra'. When the Moon passes into the Earth's penumbra or umbra, it shines less brightly, but we can still see it. The reason it is not completely hidden is that the Earth is surrounded by an atmosphere which causes the sun's rays to change direction. As a result of this phenomenon, called 'refraction', the

The **refraction of the red** rays of sunlight by the Earth's atmosphere colours the Moon as it passes through the Earth's shadow cone.

sun's rays pass at a tangent to the atmosphere, creating a cone of shadow behind the Earth, rather than a cylinder. The point of this cone of shadow is located at a distance of 268,000km from the Earth, while the average distance of the Moon is 384,000km, so the Moon is perceived as further away and therefore less bright.

Why the Moon turns red

When the eclipsed Moon passes into the Earth's umbra, it gradually turns red. There are two reasons for this. First, sunlight is not uniform: it breaks down into seven rays of different colours, ranging from blue and violet to red. These rays do not have the same wavelength, so they are refracted to different degrees by the Earth's atmosphere.

Refraction forms a cone of red light far behind the Earth, in the darkest part of the penumbra, turning the Moon reddish when it passes through this zone.

Observing an eclipse of the Moon

Lunar eclipses in Europe			
Date	enters umbra*	middle*	leaves umbra*
08.11.2003	23.32	1.18	3.04
04.05.2004	18.48	20.30	22.11
28.10.2004	1.14	3.04	4.53
17.10.2005	11.35	12.03	12.31
03.03.2007	21.30	23.20	1.11
21.02.2008	1.43	3.25	5.08
21.12.2010	6.32	8.16	10.01
* Times given in universal time (GMT).			

Lunar eclipses can be observed with the naked eye, but they are more spectacular when viewed through binoculars. The first signs are a slight loss of brightness as the Moon enters the Earth's penumbra. Then a small darker area forms on the left edge of the disc, gradually covering it completely. This shadow looks greyish at first, but then turns red. The eclipse then becomes total and the red colour covers the entire disc. As the diameter of the shadow zone is about 3 times the diameter of the Moon, the Moon may remain eclipsed in this way for almost 2 hours, after which the phenomenon unfolds in reverse; a brighter crescent appears (again on the left side of the Moon's disc), and gradually grows, until the Moon leaves the Earth's penumbra, at which point it is restored to its full brightness.

To impress Native American tribes, on 29 February 1504 Christopher Columbus announced that he would 'deprive the Moon of its light'. The following night there was a lunar eclipse, whereupon the rebellious tribes submitted to Columbus. A black Moon can be seen in the top right-hand corner of this allegorical depiction of his voyage.

Predicting natural disasters

It is understandable that we, as a society, are concerned about natural disasters that catch us by surprise because of their scale or their impact. Although risk prevention remains the best way to avert tragedy, its cost often places it beyond the grasp of all but the richest countries. It then ceases to be a national concern and becomes one that has to be addressed by the global community.

Monitoring volcanoes

Recent years have seen great advances in the prediction of volcanic eruptions. These are often preceded by measurable phenomena such as an increase in seismic activity, or dilation of the earth's crust.

Before an eruption, the disturbances in the Earth's crust caused by the movement of the molten magma create tremors that can be recorded by seismographs. Monitoring centres may also use other instruments that measure the steepness of the slopes, or the swelling of the earth due to the upward rising of magma. Accurate 3-Dimensional mapping techniques can also be used, linked to Global Positioning Systems (GPS), a satellite-based location system. These developments have made medium-term prediction much easier; however, the same cannot be said of prediction in the short term. On this timescale, the nature of the information that is required is very different: not just a determination of the exact time of any eruption, but also its size, the way materials from the eruption may flow and how this will impact on the population. Under such circumstances, the crucial decision to evacuate an area is always a difficult one. Inhabitants who may be obliged to leave their homes need to be cared for and given food and shelter, and if the situation goes on too long it may develop into a humanitarian crisis.

There are few active volcanoes that are comprehensively monitored and experience shows that some of the most serious eruptions have occurred after a long period of dormancy.

Unpredictable earthquakes

Unlike volcanic eruptions, earthquakes give no advance warning signs before they occur. Although zones where there is continuing crustal movement at plate margins have been identified, earthquakes may occur outside these areas. The risk of earthquakes is thus very hard to assess, and they are almost impossible to predict. The destructive effect of an earthquake will also depend on how deep it is generated in the Earth's crust, the nature of the materials at the surface and where it is relative to centres of population. Deep earthquakes have much of their energy removed before they reach the surface. In areas of soft surface sediment an earthquake can cause the sediment to flow, greatly increasing the likelihood of destruction. An earthquake beneath a major city will have a greater destructive effect than one in a rural area or in the offshore environment. Understanding crustal stress, the pattern of fault lines and the history of previous earthquakes are factors in assessing the risk of serious damage to property and loss of life.

One line of research involves the analysis of stress exerted along the planet's major natural fault lines. A recent study on the great North Anatolian Fault in Turkey showed that, when a large quake occurs, a significant proportion of the stress exerted in the region is not released, but simply transferred to other points along the fault in precisely defined ways. This makes it possible to identify the region where the next quake may occur. The study predicts that there will be a major earthquake in the Istanbul region within the next 20 years.

We are still a long way away from short-term prediction. In practice, the destructive effect of an earthquake involves numerous factors. Measuring the risk is difficult to do, and even more difficult to communicate successfully.

Versatile cyclones

Today it is difficult for a cyclone to form unnoticed. Cyclone monitoring is internationally co-ordinated by the World Meteorological Organization, which has designated a specialist regional centre for each ocean basin. These centres, located in Miami, Tokyo, New Delhi, Fiji and St-Denis-de-la-Réunion, have the task of detecting cyclones, monitoring how they develop and sending out warnings. Meteorological satellites can watch the birth, growth and movement of cyclones, but predicting where and when they will form and how they will develop is not easy. Depending on the atmospheric layer in which they form they may strengthen, fade, suddenly change direction or even stop in mid-Atlantic for several days, as Hurricane Mitch did in 1998. Prediction is made all the more difficult because far fewer recordings of meteorological indicators are made at sea (on buoys, boats or planes) than on land.

Flood risk

Flooding may be caused by many factors, including increased run-off due to melting snows, storms, drainage restrictions, the break-up of glaciers, tsunami, cyclones, inadequate storm water drainage in towns or the bursting of a dam or dyke. As well as flooding fields and houses, these events can unleash torrents of water or mud and may also cause landslides.

Flood prevention is difficult and costly. Until recently, the prevailing policy was to build structures which would contain rivers known to represent a danger. Many dams and dykes were built, rivers diverted to avoid zones at risk, basins dug to hold excess water and mechanisms devised for draining away rainwater in towns. Today, flood risk is considered in more global terms and at the level of catchment areas. Software is being produced to simulate the way rivers behave when snows melt or when there is particularly heavy precipitation. This should make it possible to improve management of flood risk by constantly monitoring several parameters, including the amount of snow at high altitude, the predicted weather, the river flow and the degree of saturation in the soil.

Of course, it is hard to maintain such detailed monitoring of all rivers. The first step in protection against flooding is therefore to map those places where flooding has taken place in the past; in other words, places where river deposits occur. Unlike the risk from volcanoes, earthquakes and hurricanes, flood risks can be limited by infrastructure. However, infrastructure can do little against massive flooding in densely populated areas. In this respect, global climate change and rising sea-level are a particular concern in densely populated low-lying countries such as Bangladesh. Understanding the interaction between the atmosphere, the biosphere and the geosphere, what is now termed the Earth system, is the way to better predict the changes that are inherent in living on a dynamic planet.

The Great Flood: myth or reality?

Many ancient texts describe a great flooding event in the area of the Black Sea. Today there is a growing quantity of scientific evidence suggesting that such an event really did take place.

The myth

The story of a Great Flood can be found in many civilizations on every continent, from China to North America, Africa and particularly throughout the Fertile Crescent around the rivers Tigris, Euphrates, Nile and on the western slopes of the Mediterranean coast. From Turkey to the Persian Gulf, there are stories describing a sudden flood that submerged all of the earth, sparing only a few human beings and animals that had taken refuge on a boat. The earliest version of the Great Flood to come down to us from that region is part of a text known as the Epic of Gilgamesh, written in the Akkadian language on tablets of fired clay dating from the 3rd millennium BC, and found in Mesopotamia. This is generally regarded as the source of the version best known today, the story of Noah, told in the Book of Genesis.

Science

The story of the Great Flood is one of the passages in the Bible that has intrigued scientists. Since the Middle Ages, many Christian scholars have sought to reinforce its credibility by attempting a quasi-scientific reconstruction of Noah's Ark. They were preoccupied by questions such as: what species were actually present on the boat?

How were they housed in so little space? How was daily life organized on the ark in practical terms? Later, in the 19th and 20th centuries, the historians took over the Bible story. At this time it was no longer seen as a faithful, factual account, but as a myth that had been reinterpreted in a particular religious context. It was suggested that the myth might be traced to a major historical event whose story had been passed down the generations orally. It was thought that the story of the Great Flood and Noah's Ark had its source in an exceptional rise in the levels of the Tigris and Euphrates rivers. In reality, these rivers did regularly flood, submerging the crops grown on the wide, flat plain of Mesopotamia. However, there was no evidence in the sediments for a more widespread flooding event.

The Black Sea trail

In 1996, two American experts in marine geology, William Ryan and Walter Pitman, supported by Turkish and Armenian colleagues, uncovered new evidence of a sudden rise in the level of the Black Sea 7600 years ago. Since that time, marine surveys and explorations of the seabed have provided many observations in support of this view.

The last ice age ended 12,000 years ago and the sea level, which was then about

120m lower than today, began to rise. The marine waters of the Mediterranean Sea would initially have flooded into the fresh-water Sea of Marmara. Here the waters would have been impounded, as the strait of the Bosphorus, which now links it to the Black Sea, had not yet been eroded to a depth that would permit the rising water to flow on to what is now the Black Sea. The surveys carried out by Ryan and Pitman have shown that, at that time, sea level must have been 150m higher than the level of the Euxine Sea, the freshwater lake that was to become the Black Sea. It is thought that, about 7,500 years ago, the rock barrier was breached, allowing the salty Mediterranean waters to suddenly pour into the fresh water of the lake at a rate of 1,000–2,000 cubic metres per day. This fast-flowing, debris-laden torrent would have rapidly eroded, producing the present channel, which is up to 85m wide and 145m deep.

This flooding event is also recorded in the biological record, with marine cockles and mussels replacing fresh-water shellfish. The last fresh-water shellfish dates from 8,500 years ago, and the oldest salt-water shellfish from 7,500 years ago. Between the two layers there is a substantial mix of crushed shells, the sign of an event involving very great forces. People living in the area would have fled, abandoning their wooden huts, traces of which have been found. Some of them would have sought refuge in Mesopotamia, where the myth of the Great Flood developed as we know it today.

Doubts

Not everyone accepts the scenario outlined above. The main weakness of the hypothesis is that it contradicts data from analyses of the banks of the Danube at the point where it flows into the Black Sea. This river's offshore bars show an age of 12,000 years, suggesting no sudden change in the sea level. Nonetheless, it is now beyond doubt that the fresh waters of the Black Sea were suddenly submerged by salt water about 7,500 years ago. Today there is still a 'fossil' current retaining the memory of the flood: in the Dardanelles, while the surface current flows from the Black Sea to the Mediterranean, water deeper down flows in the opposite direction.

The flood may have been less violent than Ryan and Pitman thought. In 1999 an international team led by Ali Aksu suggested that the Dnepr, Don and Danube rivers, swollen with the broken glaciers of Siberia and Northern Europe, may have caused the level of the Black Sea to rise to a height comparable to that of the Mediterranean. In this scenario they would have become joined in a less violent fashion, although a further explanation would be required for the incised Bosphorous valley. So, while the form taken by the flood may still be in doubt, its reality is not. As for the idea that the increase in the level of the Black Sea gave rise to the story of the Great Flood found in Genesis, the confirmation of this is a step that science alone cannot take.

Representation of the Great Flood on a miniature by Beatus of Liebana (Abbey of Saint-Sever, mid-11th century), Bibliothèque Nationale de France.

Glossary

[Ablation zone]
Zone in which a glacier loses mass.

[Accretion zone]
Gap between two tectonic plates into which magma flows, restoring the lithosphere.

[Accumulation zone]
Zone in which a glacier gains mass.

[Anticyclone]
Build-up of high pressure in the atmosphere; a source of downward movements.

[Astrobleme]
Crater formed when an object moving through space collides with a planet; from the Greek astron, 'star', and blema, 'wound'.

[Black ice]
Smooth, transparent layer of ice.

[Caldera]
The summit of a volcano which has collapsed due to a particularly violent eruption.

[Catchment area]
Region drained by a river and all its tributaries.

[Centrifugal force]
The force of inertia to which a rotating body is subjected, causing it to move away from the centre of its trajectory.

[Cirque]
Steep-sided, semi-circular depression that has formed above a glacier.

[Condensation]
Passing from a gaseous to a liquid state.

[Coriolis force]
Force produced by the Earth's rotation, which causes all moving objects to veer to the right in the northern hemisphere and to the left in the southern hemisphere.

[Crater]
Opening generally found at the summit of a volcano.

[Crystal]
Solid body characterized by a regular, repeated accumulation of atoms.

[Cumulonimbus]
Large, dark cloud that develops vertically and is likely to unleash a storm.

[Depression]
Atmospheric mass of low pressure; a source of rising movements.

[Elliptical]
In astronomy, this describes the elongated, curved trajectory of an object on a plane, with the Sun as one of its focuses.

[Epicentre]
Closest point on the surface to the focus of the volcano.

[Fault]
Result of a break in a group of rocks.

[Flow]
Quantity of water flowing past at any given moment in a given space of time. Flow is measured in cubic metres per second.

[Focus]
Point where the break in a group of rocks begins.

[Front]
Border zone between two atmospheric air masses of different temperatures and degrees of humidity.

[Fumarolic gas]
Gaseous emissions from a volcano.

[Geothermal]
This refers to thermal phenomena within the Earth and their study.

[Gravity]
Force responsible for the attraction of all material bodies, proportional to their mass and inversely proportional to the square of the distance between them.

[Hyperbolic]
In astronomy, this describes an elongated, curved trajectory on a plane, with the Sun as one focus and the other a point located at infinity.

[Ionosphere]
Zone of the upper atmosphere characterized by the presence of particles with an electrical charge.

[Ions]
Atoms that have lost (or gained) one or several electrons and so are not neutral but have an electrical charge.

[Light ray]
Trajectory of light moving between two points.

[Light-year]
Unit of length equivalent to 9,500 billion kilometres – the distance light travels through a vacuum in a year.

[Line of nodes]
Line joining the intersections of a moving body's orbit to a plane of reference. In the case of eclipses, this is the line of intersections of the Moon's orbital plane with the ecliptic plane.

[Lithosphere]
Outermost layer of the Earth's crust, split into tectonic plates.

[Maar]
The crater formed when rising magma hits a body of water.

[Macroseismic epicentre]
Place where the greatest intensity of an earthquake is felt.

[Magma]
Liquid formed within the Earth through the fusion of the rocks from which the planet is made.

[Mesosphere]
Layer of the Earth's atmosphere above the stratosphere, at an altitude of 40–80km.

[Meteor]
Any phenomenon (except clouds) observed in the atmosphere, particularly the luminous trail of a meteorite entering the atmosphere.

[Moraine]
Area of rocky debris carried and deposited by a glacier.

[Ocean spreading ridge]
Underwater fracture through which magma is forced, becoming part of the sea bed.

[Organic compounds]
Carbon molecules (such as aldehydes and amino acids) which are the basis of living matter.

[Plasma]
Fluid composed of electrically neutral gas molecules.

[Plinian column]
Plume of pyroclastics shaped like an umbrella, forming above the mouth of an erupting volcano when the magma contains a high proportion of dissolved gas and has been compressed by passing through a narrow chimney.

[Pumice]
Very light, porous volcanic rock.

[Pyroclastics]
Projected debris emitted by a volcano, including dust, ash (2mm in diameter), lapilli (2–64mm) and bombs or blocks (more than 64mm).

[Refraction]
1. Change of direction of a wave passing from one medium to another. Sunlight is refracted by the Earth's atmosphere, with each ray changing its path differently according to its wavelength.

2. Phenomenon in which a wave rolls in on itself, due to the different speeds of its various parts located at different heights.

[Rift valley]
Valley where the Earth's crust has collapsed due to tensions in the lithosphere.

[Seismology]
The science of earthquakes.

[Subduction zone]
Zone where one lithospheric plate (generally oceanic) slides under another (continental in most cases).

[Supercooling]
Phenomenon in which a substance remains in a liquid state below the temperature at which it would normally solidify.

[Tsunami]
Tidal wave caused by the sudden disturbance of a water column, resulting from an event such as an earthquake or volcanic eruption.

[Typhoon]
The name for cyclones in the Far East.

[Volcanic mechanism]
Matter surrounding the volcano and involved in its functioning.

[Zeolite]
Natural, porous silicate of volcanic origin; from the Ancient Greek meaning 'moving stone'.

Useful websites

BBC Weather
http://www.bbc.co.uk/weather/

British Antarctic Survey
http://www.antarctica.ac.uk/

British Geological Survey
http://www.bgs.ac.uk/

Earth Observatory
http://earthobservatory.nasa.gov/

Earthquake Hazards (BGS)
http://www.earthquakes.bgs.ac.uk/

Earthquake Hazards (USGS)
http://earthquake.usgs.gov/

European Space Agency
http://www.esa.int/export/esaCP/index.html

How Stuff Works
http://www.howstuffworks.com/index.htm

Jet Propulsion Lab (CIT)
http://www.jpl.nasa.gov/

MET Office
http://www.met-office.gov.uk/index.html

Montserrat Volcano Observatory
http://www.mvo.ms/

NASA
http://www.nasa.gov/home/index.html

National Snow and Ice Data Centre
http://nsidc.org/

Natural History Museum
http://www.nhm.ac.uk/

Norsk BreMuseum
http://www.bre.museum.no/

Scott Polar Research Institute
http://www.spri.cam.ac.uk/

Space Weather
http://www.spaceweather.com/

United States Geological Survey
http://www.usgs.gov/

Volcano World
http://volcano.und.nodak.edu/vw.html

Suggestions for further reading

GENERAL TITLES

Fortey, R, *The Earth: An Intimate History*, HarperCollins, London, 2004

McGuire, B, *Raging Planet: earthquakes, volcanoes and the tectonic threat to life on earth*, Apple Press, Hove, 2002

Redfern, R, *Origins: the evolution of continents, oceans and life*, Cassell, London, 2002

Ritchie, D and Gates, A E, *Encyclopedia of Earthquakes and Volcanoes*, 2nd edn, Facts on File, New York, 2001

Scarth, A, *Savage Earth: The Dramatic Story of Volcanoes and Earthquakes*, HarperCollins, London, 2001

Van Rose, S, *Earth*, 2nd edn, Dorling Kindersley, London, 2000

EARTHQUAKES

Ganeri, A and Phillips, M, *Earth-shattering Earthquakes* (Horrible Geography series), Scholastic, London, 2000

Van Rose, S, *Earthquakes: our trembling planet*, Earthwise Publications (British Geological Survey), Keyworth, 1997

METEORITES

Hutchinson, R and Graham, A, *Meteorites*, The Natural History Museum, London, 2000

VOLCANOES

Clarkson, P and Houston, D, *Volcanoes*, Voyageur Press, Stillwater, MN, 2002

Ganeri, A, *Violent Volcanoes* (Horrible Geography series), Scholastic, London, 1999

Putnam, J and Van Rose, S, *Volcano*, Dorling Kindersley, London, 2002

WEATHER SYSTEMS & RELATED

Cosgrove, B, *Weather*, Dorling Kindersley, London, 2002

Ganeri, A and Phillips, M, *Raging Rivers and Odious Oceans* (Horrible Geography series), Scholastic, London, 2001

Ganeri, A, *Stormy Weather* (Horrible Geography series), Scholastic, London, 1999

Gordon, J, *Glaciers*, Colin Baxter Photography, Grantown-on-Spey, 2002

Macquitty, M, *Desert*, Dorling Kindersley, London, 1994

Maslin, M, *Global Warming*, Colin Baxter Photography, Grantown-on-Spey, 2002

Mogil, H M, *Tornadoes*, Colin Baxter Photography, Grantown-on-Spey, 2001

Index

Page numbers in *italics* refer to illustrations. **Bold** type indicates pages where the topic is dealt with in some detail.

Illustration credits

Photographs

Drawings and computer graphics